The Wealthy
Intentional
Entrepreneur

How to Build Financial Wealth

One Step at a Time

SECOND EDITION

NATALYA ITU, CPA

BAILEY'S
PUBLISHING

Second Edition, 2019

The Wealthy Intentional Entrepreneur: How to Build Financial Wealth One Step at a Time / by Natalya Itu

Published by Bailey's Publishing, LLC
Aurora, CO

To my parents,
thank you for your
great life lessons.
I love you both!

Contents

Introduction

DEAR AMBITIOUS ENTREPRENEUR, welcome to your exciting journey of intentional entrepreneurship! The word intentional became my go-to word in the past few years as I started thinking about how to improve my business to a level of performance where it could function effectively without me. I wanted to make sure that both my clients and my employees would still be happy in my absence. The truth is that a business cannot be built without a clear vision. You have to have an idea of where you want your business to end up not only financially, but what positive impact and legacy it will leave after you decide to exit it. You should also have an idea of how it should operate in optimum circumstances. In other words, formulating a clear vision for the future is what helps lead the processes necessary to your success. When you started your business, it was an act from the heart. It was your passion about your goals that led you on this journey to entrepreneurship. Your enthusiasm and skills are there to help along the way. You love what you do. Whether you enjoy the actual work or not, you thrive on delivering the services that you provide or the products that you offer.

> *"The truth is that a business cannot be built without a clear vision."*

There is a wonderful energy that comes with starting something new and spending every waking hour getting it off the ground. This is all well and good until your business begins to grow as planned, but most of the time by default. During this growth, there will be a moment in which reality hits you. It might be a moment during a vacation or a moment during ill health. It is a moment when you realize that you don't have a business—you have a job. Some people are content with this. Some people prefer not to grow their business beyond a certain point. My mother, for example, used to clean houses for many years. She did so without any help. Not because she couldn't have used the help, but because she preferred to keep her life simple. She never made business cards for her business or bothered with any other type of marketing. She was happy with the simple way she earned her money and thankful that her daughter the CPA was able to help declare her earnings and file taxes for her. This, however, is not a true business. This is self-employment. For some people, this state of self-employment is perfect. My mom had found her sweet spot, where she was content with the amount of money she was making, so why bother to change?

However, if your goal is to own a seven-figure business, make an impact within your company and in the community, then you must begin by becoming an *intentional* entrepreneur. One that is committed to empowering yourself to take bigger actions, expanding your thinking and risk tolerance, and growing your business to its maximum potential.

Let's start this intentional journey together...

CHAPTER **1**

First Steps in Building Financial Wealth

IF YOUR goal is to grow your business to a seven-figure level, then you need to be open to change. Whether it's changing your mindset or the way you run your business, growing a seven-figure, successful, and profitable business requires intentional thinking and planning. In reality, you can manage your five to low six figure business without any help, big vision, systems or people. However, the landscape will start changing when you want to grow your business into seven figures. At this level, it becomes absolutely necessary to get help, create systems in writing, be able to manage cash flow, check people's productivity, and maintain a clean business track record.

When I started my CPA practice in 2010, it felt like the only professional knowledge I had was preparing tax returns and bookkeeping tasks using QuickBooks software. I did not even know how to run payroll or file payroll reports at this time. I had never been given an opportunity to learn how to do payroll while working in various CPA firms. This was due to the fact that payroll is the least expensive task, so CPAs were not assigned to it. This meant that I had to learn how to run payroll the hard way, all by myself and making several mistakes along the way. Leaving my day-to-day job was risky. I chose to step out of my comfort zone and start my own practice since I knew it would be my only way out of the rat race. So, when I started my firm, I just wanted to work for myself and make a lot of money. This all sounds nice and easy on paper, but in reality, owning a business typically means a lot of work and surviving with a low cash flow in the beginning.

Plan on not making a substantial amount of money at first, and even less when you work for yourself and you are the only one who is working. In order to build a seven-figure business, you need to leverage your business model so that other people on your team can do the work as well. *"You need to think leverage!"* The best way to establish a routine and good workflow is by keeping tabs on your systems and processes. You need to think leverage! I will discuss this concept more thoroughly in the later chapters. Meanwhile, let's talk numbers and how it can affect your financial future.

Planning for your tax liability and reviewing your numbers is a very critical moment at any point in life. As a business owner living with intention, investing your money and building financial wealth should be one of the most important items on your list. Over the past few years, numerous overarching changes have been implemented that directly impact businesses across the U.S. The tax world is getting trickier to navigate, leaving just as much room for error as it does for opportunity. It is because of these changes and the complexity involved in understanding financial institutions and processes that I would like to offer you a comprehensive tax-time and accounting checklist.

This checklist is sure to uncover a few unexpected tax savings for you. Each tip comes with expert insights that interpret into possible savings as well as additional income. Some of the items might not be relevant to you at this time, but they could offer savings if implemented in the future. Depending on where you are in your life, consideration of these items can help you develop an effective manageable financial plan that can grow your net worth to the next level.

Building a successful business, as well as your financial prosperous future, takes more than just discipline. These goals require specific action plans, a positive mindset, and unbreakable determination. I believe this book will help you gain clarity towards building your prosperous future!

Now, let us begin.

Making an Intentional Decision to Increase
Your Net Worth in One Year

Congratulations on your interest in improving your financial standing and planning for a better financial future that could increase your net worth by the end of the year. As with any change you make in your life, the very first step of the process should be to make an intentional decision about building your successful financial future. Financial wealth is always built with intention; you cannot become rich by default. Those who achieve financial success have set their intentions to do so. Even lottery ticket winners have to buy a ticket first! Setting specific investment goals requires both effort and attention. This includes diligent steps of creating a variety of investment vehicles, following your plan, reviewing it, and taking corrective action. Although this process is beneficial, it also requires getting out of your comfort zone and facing your fears face to face. In order to get different, more positive results in your life, you need to do something that you have not done before—something you might even be uncomfortable with.

"Financial wealth is always built with intention."

Most of the millionaire clients at our firm have three main investment sources through which their net worth increases. We call this investment a "trifecta," or the three-legged stool. One leg stands for business ownership, the second for availability and consistent contribution to growing retirement accounts or life insurance policies, and the third one stands for holding real estate investments with positive cash flow as well as increasing equity. Diversifying your portfolio with various types of investments is not only beneficial for tax planning and reduction of your tax bill, but also helps with hedging risk of asset performance and cash flow availability.

Action Plan to Begin Your Intentional Journey:

1. Your first assignment is to create a list of the assets you own and determine their fair market value. Feel free to use *Table 1* in the Appendix for reference.

To find the equity of your real estate investments, subtract the current liability up to date from the Fair Market Value of the asset. An easy way to find the fair market value of your assets is by using real estate websites such as Zillow.com. You can also ask your local real estate professional to research what price similar properties in your neighborhood are selling for. Unless you need to establish your exact net worth number for loan origination purposes or estate/trust planning, don't spend too much time or money on appraisals. Although you can order official appraisal reports at any time, unless you plan to sell the properties in the very near future, I would not recommend spending money on it. Fair values are constantly adapting to current market trends, so they never remain constant too long.

As far as stocks or retirement accounts, these figures are available to you every month on the brokerage reports.

You can simply pull records from your accounts or ask your financial advisor to do so on your behalf. With this in mind, if you do not already have a financial advisor as a part of your professional team, then I would highly encourage you to hire one. We work with a few very good financial advisors on a regular basis. Don't be shy to ask us for a referral.

How can you evaluate how much your business is worth? This can be done by hiring a professional, licensed and certified Business Valuation Specialist. Perhaps you would need to know the worth of your business for a loan or future transition of ownership. You can do research on your industry to better understand how sales price is calculated for your particular business. This task also proves beneficial as it not only allows you to see how much your business is worth, but also what you need to do to increase your business worth. Please refer to and complete *Table 2* in the Appendix to evaluate your Business Net Worth.

By filling out *Table 2* honestly, you will gain an enormous amount of clarity about your business health. If you plan to sell your business in the future, it's crucial to plan for it now, even if the sale will not take place for another 3 to 5 years. If you decide to sell, spend some time clarifying what you need to do and determine what action steps you can take right now. Action is required sooner rather than right before you decide to sell it. I am not suggesting to cook the numbers in the slow cooker and allow yourself to be overwhelmed by the prospect. Instead, I am suggesting that you watch your expenses, cash flow movements, your debt and your retained earnings. You don't want to have negative retained earnings on your balance sheet. Negative retained earnings may indicate that your business is losing money, you could be taking too much in shareholder's distributions or it could be an excess of your basis financial interest of the company, in other words showing that your business may be in debt. Healthy, positive retained earnings, which is the same as your business net worth, must always be a positive number. It would be wise to hire a Chief Financial Officer (CFO) or a Fractional CFO who specializes in small businesses to make these analyses for you. They are experts in their field and would be able to help you figure out your financial statements and how you can improve them. Our firm offers a package known as Strategic CFO. In this package, you will meet with members of the firm on a quarterly basis to gain clarity as to where your business stands. We will also help you create an action plan for the next year to help you reach your goals and improve your business financial health.

2. Now, determine the net worth of your personal assets by adding the fair market value (FMV) of each of your assets together and subtracting any liabilities—including outstanding loans and other debts. In other words, your net worth is the FMV of what you own minus what is owed.

Examples of Common Personal Assets can be:

- **Your home.** Find the current market value of your home. If you've owned your home for a few years, it may be significantly higher than the original purchase price, depending on whether you bought it at high or low market cycle.

- **Other Real Estate investments.** Find the current market value of other properties such as a second home, vacation home, time share or other real estate shared with business partners or friends (that is for personal use only). Find the current market value of any second homes, rental properties, commercial buildings or undeveloped land that you own. (As a side note, I would not recommend to buy a time share! Airbnb is a much better deal when you plan your vacation!)

- **Automobiles.** Determine the FMV of any automobiles you own. Do not include leased vehicles in your valuation. Most likely, your vehicle will have a negative net worth. That means that you owe more money for them than what they are worth. It is recommended not to buy highly-depreciable assets without a down payment or paying cash for them. This is because in the very worst cases, the loan from the previous vehicle can roll over into the new vehicle loan when the vehicle is traded in. It is almost impossible to get out of debt from this scenario, as the debt "snow ball" just keeps accumulating with the passing years.

- **Other vehicles.** Boats, campers, RVs, motorcycles and other specialty vehicles hold significant monetary value and add to your net worth. On the other side, if you still owe money on them, they will significantly decrease your net worth.

- **Jewelry.** Valuable gems and precious metals, such as gold, can fluctuate in value over time. Research their current FMV annually as they may have appreciated over time.

- **Miscellaneous.** You might also possess some precious metals, works of art, intellectual property, etc.

Now that we've discussed your assets, let's talk about your liabilities. Let's get into the details about how much you currently owe for some of your assets. If you owe money on real estate (personal, business or investment) please pull your last month's mortgage statements to determine what your remaining liability is on these accounts. I would also suggest that you compare it with your amortization schedule to see how much of your monthly payment currently goes towards your principal amount reduction and how much goes towards your loan interest.

If you cannot remember all of your liabilities, then contact a credit reporting bureau. Credit bureaus will have a detailed list of your outstanding loans. You should also pull your credit report on an annual basis to compare the information on your report to what you know you have on the bank statements.

Do you have business lines of credit? Do you owe money to the IRS or other state tax agencies? What about your personal debt, such as medical bills, credit cards, student loans, auto loans? Do you owe interest on these loans? Do you have a plan to tackle your debt and do you know the date by which you plan to become either debt-free or at least free of bad debt?

These are all important questions to ask when reviewing your annual credit report.

While on the topic of debt, what is debt anyway? Usually debt can be considered as the amount owed that you've accumulated by purchasing assets over time. These typically decrease rapidly in value. Not surprisingly, having too much debt is harmful and could impede you from reaching your investment goals, as it takes away from your revenue when calculating your net worth. At this time, please go to the this Appendix and take a look at *Table 4*. This Table will help you identify unsecured debt and will provide you with an action plan to reduce it.

3. **As a feel-good exercise, I would like you to create a list of your non-financial assets.**

These should include your education, experiences, your employees and any other assets that will help you to expedite your personal or business growth process. Some of these assets might be almost impossible to put a financial number on, but I believe it is still a good reminder exercise that can help boost your self-esteem. It might also help remind you of all the resources you have available and will help you feel thankful for what you have so far. If you have your business systems in writing and your employees use them, this is also considered an invaluable asset. This is how franchisers make money—by selling predictable business models developed via systematization. Once you systematize and implement your business systems on a daily basis, you can truly predict results. Not only does creating and following systems deliver consistency in your business, but it can also help you make educated predictions as to how much cash your business will generate in the future. Possibly, it can even help predict what kind of growth your business is headed towards.

For your next exercise, go ahead and make some notes of how you can use your non-financial resources to increase your financial net worth. Think of ways you can leverage these assets to generate additional streams of revenue. For example, perhaps you're about to breakthrough in your business. This might be because you finally have a great team in place, or maybe you have a substantial client list, or maybe you have created some new connections which have expanded your networking opportunities. These non-financial assets vary greatly in tangible value, but they can end up having one of the largest impacts on your bottom line revenue. Just think about the potential growth a marketing email campaign or new program can generate for your business. If you are successful in leveraging your non-financial assets, then obtaining additional revenue should become easier and faster than ever before.

Don't underestimated the power of your non-financial resources; they are what will propel your success. Your goal is to learn more about how to leverage and use these resources more often to achieve even greater financial results. The process of identifying your non-financial assets increases your confidence, which ultimately increases your earning potential. At this time please refer to *Table 5* in the Appendix to list all of the qualifications you are proud of. Don't forget to note your unique abilities and mention what you're really good at!

4. Now, the final action plan for this year is the decision to increase your net worth.

After you put all assets and liabilities in place and subtract your assets from your liabilities, you will be getting a positive or a negative number. This number represents your net worth. It can be a positive number or it can be a negative number. The negative net worth would mean that your liabilities are higher than your assets. If this is the case, I would recommend consulting with a professional about your debt reduction plan as well as investment strategies. By the way, if you had a cancellation of debt and you have a negative net worth, or had at the time of debt cancellation, your cancelled debt might not be a taxable item up to the amount of insolvency. For example, if you have a negative net worth of $5,000 and you had a cancellation of credit card debt in the amount of $8,000, only $3,000 would be considered as taxable income to you as a cancellation of debt, because you are considered to be insolvent up to $5,000. Sometimes being broke can help to save money on taxes but it is not recommended as a long-term tax reducing strategy.

In any situation, you should always be focusing on building a positive net worth with positive cash flow. Make a decision to increase your net worth by the end of the year. Reasonably estimate how much you want to increase it by and start working on it. Some people focus on short-term projects or solutions, but you should remember that building positive net worth is a long-term process. Therefore, any decision you make in terms of investments should be a long-term decision.

"Make a decision to increase your net worth by the end of the year."

CHAPTER **2**

Strategies to Increase Business Net Worth

WHAT ARE the ways you can start building either a positive net worth or increase your already positive net worth? Remember, net worth comes from several investment sources, and therefore, you should also focus on several ways to increase it.

I believe every one of us goes through financial difficulties at some point in our lives. I was no exception. Back in 2007, in just a matter of two years, I lost my job and had my Florida property foreclosed. I also took time off to study for a CPA exam and decided to move to CO. So many things were happening during this time. Needless to say, I was in debt. However, even with all of these obstacles in my life, I still decided to start my business during this time. When I met with my first financial advisor, I wanted to pass off my business since the stress and struggles of my business were beginning to catch up to me. I wanted to just be rid of it all and simply contribute $100 per month to my Roth IRA. To all this she simply replied, "Natalya, just pay off your debt!" I had a lot of it. Student loans, car loans, lots of credit card debt. Her simple little comment recuperated my strength and pushed me to keep going. I am sharing this personal story with you to offer you courage and hope if you are in debt at this moment like I once was. Don't be discouraged—work on building a plan and pay it off!

Here are some tips that helped me…

Debt Reductions

First of all, create a debt reduction plan. Refer to *Table 4* in the Appendix to help with the following exercise.

List all of your debts from smallest to largest and start a plan to slowly repay each one. Don't worry about interest rates—just start with the more manageable debt first to get your self-esteem momentum going. Before you do that, make sure you have savings to cover at least two-months-worth of your expenses overall (both business and personal). Personally, I used Dave Ramsey's Financial Peace University when I started my own debt repayment program. I highly recommend it. I was listening to the CDs on a daily basis. It aligned and got me focused on paying off my debt as soon as I could!

Make a list of your debt and create a plan to pay it off. Include the projected payments and timeframe for repayment, including accrued interest. Create a debt repayment forecast to reflect cash outflow for proper cash management and planning. The key is to have a deadline as well as not to get more debt on one account by trying to pay it off

"Always push yourself the extra mile to get rid of your debt once and for all."

on other debt accounts. At this time, please use *Table 4* in the Appendix to calculate your unsecured debt. Always push yourself the extra mile to get rid of your debt once and for all.

Cash Flow Management and Savings

If you are employed by someone, there are always many options to obtain some more cash flow. You could focus on making yourself more efficient, be more proactive and become indispensable in the eyes of your boss, which can increase your chances when asking for a raise. If the time allows, you could also get a second job, even if it is just part time. See if you can get paid per project, verses hourly. Change employers (not the best option, especially when I am all for being loyal), as you can get more of a raise that way. Get extra gigs from Fiverr or Upwork. Don't limit yourself.

If you have a business, then one good way to increase cash flow is by implementing and enforcing good collection policies. How does your business collect cash? What do you do when a customer is behind on payments? What are your cash collection systems and procedures? Do you know when your cash balance fluctuates and why? How can you improve your cash flow? A few options can include encouraging customers to prepay for your services, offering monthly subscriptions to your customers, making sure that collection of cash at the time of services being performed is enforced, and having the ability to accept all credit cards, etc. These should all be detailed in a formal policy or business handbook. Make sure to brainstorm some ideas and act on them. Always add more value to your customers and become their trusted partner and advisor, so you are on their priority list of payments.

Sales Strategies

What are some ways in which you can increase your sales? Are you in the growth mode of your business? Have you increased the prices on your services lately? Are you charging fair market prices, below or over? Who is your ideal client? What do they think of your prices? Keep these questions in mind when brainstorming ideas.

I always suggest for business owners to not only create a budget (spending report, as I call it), but also sales forecasts. In forecasts, you need to determine your predictable future sales. Once you have this estimated future sales number, then you can divide it by the number of months it will take you to get there and compare it to your current sales numbers to see if you are on track.

For example, at our firm, we use weekly scorecards to compare actual performance with the goals taken from forecasts. This helps us to see if we are on target to achieve our established sales, as well as view other business key performance indicators.

If you are employed by someone else, are you being fairly compensated for your time and expertise? Are you learning new skills and implementing new ways of improving your employer's business? Are you investing in yourself so that ultimately everyone in your organization benefits? If the answer is yes to any or all of the above, then it is time to ask for a raise or partially modify your compensation to commission-based. You need to think of ways to make more money. Once again, refer to *Table 5* in the Appendix where you listed your non-financial assets to gain more confidence and increase your self-esteem.

Optimizing Efficiency

Efficiency in business is key for long-term success. First, you need to ensure that your business is operating at peak performance while

> *"Efficiency in business is key for long-term success."*

managing expenses. How can you tell that your business operates efficiently? Do you know your team's performance? Does your business have a way to measure that performance efficiency? How can you make your business more efficient via the use of technology, team training, accountability tools and inspiration? Brainstorm three ways to increase and improve efficiency in your business.

While you increase productivity, you must manage costs. Just because a new piece of equipment could expedite a process, does it automatically mean it's worth the cost? Do you review your income statement on a regular basis? Do you compare it with your budget amounts? Do you budget in the first place? Perhaps there are expenses that should either be reduced or eliminated all together? Brainstorm and generate three ideas on expense reduction. If you already feel confused and frustrated or overwhelmed, feel free to contact our office—we would love to help you!

Real Estate

Now, let's talk about real estate. If you are not passionate about real estate, feel free to skip this part of the chapter. However, I believe that investment in real estate should be a significant part of your investment portfolio. Additionally, real estate investment is a great leverage tool in general, because real estate can help utilize significant leverage with other people's money. For example, when you buy an investment property, banks usually require somewhere from 5% to 20% in down payment (depending on the loan program and type of property purchased). Appreciation in real estate is a great benefit, as is positive cash flow. As long as your property generates positive cash flow, meaning your income from rents exceeds all expenses and monthly loan repayment amounts, you should consider it to be a good investment. Don't forget to count into the equation the depreciation expense. What this means is that when you place your real estate property for rent, you need to depreciate it over 27.5 years (residential rental) according to the IRS Tax Code. Don't forget to separate partial costs of the house from the costs of the land itself. The depreciation expense will be subtracted for tax purposes to come up to net rental income; however, the depreciation expense is considered a non-cash expense. The IRS requires you to take a depreciation expense when you place your property for rent.

What does all of this mean? Basically, when you buy a rental property (such as a single-family home, condo, apartment complex, etc.), you want to make sure that you receive a positive cash flow. That means that rental income should exceed your monthly expenses (loan payment, interest on the loan, HOA, insurance, real estate taxes, etc.) There are definitely other factors to consider as well. For example, the real estate appreciation factors (location and condition of the property for that matter), economical factors, etc. As long as you have cash left after your tenants have paid you, your investment would be considered acceptable.

Action plan for building a stronger real estate portfolio:

1. Keep cash flow positive.

Remember—positive cash flow is king! Are you in position to buy real estate properties? Do you have enough cash to put an acceptable amount into a down payment?

Before you buy a real estate property, make sure you think about its purpose: is it going to be a rental property or a vacation home? When are you planning to sell it? If you are planning to buy property in a different state, then you must first consider the market there, appreciation

"Positive cash flow is king!"

trends as well as travel and management costs associated with managing property long-distance. Do intensive research for pricing in that area. For example, I live in Colorado. At the time I am writing this book, the real estate market is insane. Most real estate property sellers in Colorado obtain several offers just within hours after the property goes on the market, even with the prices typically being several thousand dollars higher than the asking price. In contrast, I also have a property in Florida. As of this moment, we are in the process of selling our condo there. We had two showing cancellations within two days and the property has been on the market for over a year. I believe that when I bought this property a few years ago, I applied the same mindset from the purchase experience in Colorado. I was in a hurry and offered the asking price, which my agent decreased by a couple of thousand dollars. Knowing what I know now, I realize that I overpaid at least five thousand dollars for this property. Don't make the same mistake and do some extensive research of the market before you buy. Make sure to ask and interview agents, and most importantly, don't rush—especially when the market is cold (buyer's market).

Here is another important point: When you buy a property, buy what you can afford while maintaining a positive cash flow component. If it is a rental property, make sure you have at least $100 to your name by the end of the month. Don't buy something you need to feed with your cash derived from somewhere else. Remember, you should strive to buy an asset, not a liability!

2. Improvements and repairs.

Do not underestimate the amount of work you might need to do on the property. Real estate often needs mainte-nance, sometimes unexpected. Save enough money and keep those reserved funds in a special bank account to cover both emergencies and unexpected remodels and repair issues.

3. Understanding taxation derived from real estate transactions.

It might feel, in the short-run, that real estate is not a good investment due to this tie-up of assets. That's because real estate investment is meant to be a long-term strategy! No wonder why the IRS tax code particularly discerns real estate investors (long-term focused) from real estate dealers (short-term focused, usually property flippers). The net income derived from the sale of real estate is subject to an ordinary income tax rate with a self-employment tax component for professionals who flip houses by buying them, fixing and quickly selling them. These transactions usually take less than one year and happen several times per year. On the other hand, the IRS tax code does encourage long-term investment in real estate (holding real estate properties for at least one year and one day or longer), and categorizes that income from the real estate sale as a long-term capital gains transaction, subject to long-term capital gains rates (somewhere between 0-20% in taxes) depending on your ordinary income tax rate.

In my practice I work with a lot of different types of real estate investors. Some of them are considered real estate dealers, some of them are real estate investors. As I already mentioned in the previous paragraph, real estate dealers are professionals whose intent is to purchase property, quickly fix it and resell it at a higher price. The IRS considers these people real estate dealers and categorizes their real estate activities' income as derived from self-employment. There is no doubt that dealers pay much higher in taxes. Therefore, before you begin your real estate investment career, think about what appeals to you and include tax consequences in your decision-making process. If you are a dealer and your passion is to fix and flip real estate property, create your LLC and convert it into an S-corporation. Run your business as an S-corporation to save money on self-employment taxes. Our firm can help you with that and to stay in compliance with IRS rules.

4. Know your classification.

Again, there are tests to determine whether the real estate professional should be classified as a dealer (thereby paying higher taxes) or a real estate investor. Even if you had one property and sold it in less than one year after purchasing it, it does not mean that you are automatically classified as a real estate dealer. I guess the best question to ask would be this: What was my intent when I purchased this real estate property? Did I want to hold it and rent it but my circumstances changed, or did I want to "flip" it even before I decided to buy it?

5. Utilize tax incentives.

There are also other tax incentives available to real estate investors, such as the code 1031 exchange. With this exchange, you can sell your old investment property and find a replacement property and pay no taxes on asset appreciation by utilizing the 1031 technique. 1031 Exchange is the IRS tax code that allows real estate investors (not dealers) to sell their investment real estate property and purchase a new one, usually bigger and better, for business (not personal use) by following a specified set of rules to defer income from appreciation of the old property by carrying it and applying it to the new property. You need to hire a third party intermediary and follow a set of rules, such as you have 45 days to identify the new replacement property and 180 days to complete the transaction (purchase a new replacement property), while proceeds from the sale of the old property are in the possession of the intermediary. With the current significant increase on real estate prices in Colorado, it is becoming a very popular technique to stay ahead of the game. Investors, by being able to keep the significant amount of tax savings, gain advantage to buy better quality replacement properties.

If you are certain that you want to buy, fix and sell real estate properties right away, I would suggest to talk to a CPA to find a better tax strategy for your business. Since being a dealer is considered a self-employed business activity with self-employed tax consequences, converting your business into an S-corporation and following a specific set of rules can be a solution for your tax-saving strategies.

Whichever way you choose to build and increase your in-vestment portfolio, real estate provides one of the great vehicles for it. I agree that this type of investment is not for everyone. Just follow what you feel more familiar and comfortable with.

Invest in Yourself First

Always invest in yourself! Increase your technical knowledge, stretch your mindset for possibilities of doing more and being more! Socialize with like-minded, driven individuals, create mastermind groups and support each other to achieve to your highest potential!

"Always invest in yourself!"

Each individual net worth number will be different, but I would suggest making up an ideal number that is just right for you and your business, and then determine its source (via business, real estate, stocks, bonds, investments or debt reduction). Then set a date and make an effort to change your net worth for more in that amount of time.

> **Action plan for investing in yourself:**
>
> 1. **Set up automatic deposit.**
>
> Set up an automatic withdrawal from your checking account to send a set amount of money to your Roth or Traditional IRA. The secret is to get started! You can start small; as long as you move along and keep it going, you will be further than you thought you would be. Go for it! Meet with your financial advisor and discuss your retirement investment strategies.
>
> Maximize your 401K contributions. Depending on your age, perhaps you might want to contribute some of your money to Roth 401K and some to a regular, tax deductible 401K. Always have some type of retirement plan available through your business. It is a good attraction tool for high quality employees as well as tax savings techniques for business owners.
>
> 2. **Build your intellectual program.**
>
> We live in an information age and we invest a great deal in different types of coaching and mastermind groups. Have you considered creating and selling your personal

program by using the latest applications, phone video features, software and other technologies? I was watching Shark Tank the other day while at the gym, and was amazed by how many businesses are creating sales via the Internet! At my firm we get clients that were intrigued by our YouTube channel videos, or happened to stumble upon the company website, or saw one of our events on Facebook, or even just happened to Google the closest CPA firm to their business. We receive reviews at all of these places and most of the time all these extra clients are not even being targeted intentionally! This is one of the newest but very popular ways to increase your business income and own your own educational program. You can set it up completely evergreen, meaning you would not have to manually maintain or sell it. Technology and systems will handle it for you. I agree it can be intimidating at the beginning, but it is totally feasible. How many people do you know who make money off the Internet? I know a few and they are very successful. Some of them are our clients.

As we discussed in the introductory chapter, in order to build a seven-figure business, you need to have people, systems and a million-dollar mindset. Let's talk about people.

Let's talk about which professionals you need to have on your team to keep you accountable and knowledgeable, and how to communicate with them (what questions to ask, set up expectations as well as get encouragement). Yes, I did say get encouragement! Building a positive net worth is not an easy process; you want to make sure you socialize with like-minded individuals, as you do need to stay focused and motivated to get to your goal.

"Surround yourself with people who keep you looking towards the future rather than the past."
—Dan Sullivan, Strategic Coach®

Assembling Your Business Advisory Team

It is no secret that in order to achieve personal and financial success, you need to have a team of professionals on your side. The same goes for your business. You cannot build a successful six-figure business (moreover, a seven-figure business) without working with bright, successful, smart, positive and uplifting people. The secret to success is in the level and psychology of the people you communicate consistently with. Are you communicating with open-minded, risk takers? People who are focused on positive results and the desire to achieve something meaningful in life? Or perhaps you surround yourself with people who are constantly blaming others for their failures, are not willing to take risks, nor have a clear vision or goals in mind? Select your friends and team members wisely; not only for their professional designation but also for their psychological desires. Do you have anything in common with your friends? Are they putting you down or lifting you up? Are you happy to share your successes with them? If so, they are important assets in your life—treasure them, leverage them, and keep growing these positive connections in your life.

Relationship building is not just important for your personal life; you should focus on building a team of professionals who will help you in your business as well. When you are in business, you definitely need a CPA (Certified Public Accountant), Business Attorney, Estate and Trust Attorney, Real Estate Attorney, Banker, Mortgage Broker, Insurance Broker, Real Estate Broker, HR and Payroll Specialist, and a very successful and ambitious business coach. These individuals have years of experience in the niche aspects that make up your complex organization. They can work with you to understand your goals and apply their respective expertise to help you reach them more effectively. This professional relationship building experience will also help you build a network of strong referral partners. You and your professional team will learn from each other's strengths, weaknesses, and unique skills, allowing you to confidently send business to them as well as receive business that they are confident to refer to you. It's a win-win for all parties involved. Please refer to *Table 6* in the Appendix for this exercise. Here is a little homework to help you get started:

1. Make a list of your referral partners and team members in your business.
2. Create a schedule to meet with these people regularly, at least once per quarter, and invite them for lunch or coffee.
3. Make a list of potential referral partners and team members who you need to meet in order to increase your

business success. Make a commitment to meet these people by asking other friends for referrals.

4. Create a networking calendar for the entire year and schedule at least one meeting per week with your referral partner, your client, or a friend to deepen your business relationships and ultimately create more success for you and your business.

5. I even encourage you to create your own mastermind group with uplifting, inspiring people to share your challenges, victories and your business progress. Accountability is really important when it comes to moving your business to the next level.

With that said, choose your employees wisely as well. Make sure that the people you surround yourself with, as well as other people on your team, are on the same wavelength—meaning that they share your vision and core values, as well as your success!

Now let's get to the nitty-gritty of things by discussing your financial situation in your business and ways to improve it. Remember, business ownership is not a sprint but rather a marathon. It is a never-ending, constantly evolving personal growth experience. Yes, I did say "personal growth." Business ownership and personal growth are interconnected. When mistakes are made, you learn from them. You also gain confidence and hopefully the ability to reflect on things that don't work. All of this helps you gain clarity into your own

"Your business net-worth is a direct reflection of your self-worth!"

personal development. How do you deal with fears and uncertainty? Are you afraid of rejection? Do you remember the time when you were afraid to charge your fair value for your services because you were afraid to not have enough clients only to find out that the clients you got were not your ideal clients? I enjoy the process of business ownership. I believe that it makes people stronger psychologically, mentally, and spiritually. Your business net-worth is a direct reflection of your self-worth!

If you feel uncomfortable charging your fair market price for your services, incurring additional investment expenditures, or developing a product or service that you are not sure how it will be accepted by the public, you are stepping out of your comfort zone. Congratulations! I remember when I had anxiety about payroll day just to realize how much money was coming out of my business to pay for salaries, taxes, insurances, and rent. I was not used to paying that much, and it was uncomfortable at first. **The key is not to shrink yourself and your accomplishments by going back, but to expand even more, grow your sales, your people, and your customer base, so you can make more and have a greater impact.** Growth—personal and business—occurs outside of your comfort zone! This is why I said that business ownership is a great way to improve your personal development.

Before you go out and expand your business to its maximum potential, start by doing some math and go over some numbers. Make a budget and a forecast to make sure you have enough cash to sustain your growth.

Now it is time to discuss the financial parts of your business!

CHAPTER 3

How to Approach
Business Finances

THANKS TO many years of working with small business owners in terms of their accounting and tax needs, I can almost always predict when the business owner is going to make or lose money. I can sometimes even tell how much people make just by talking to them about how they lead and treat their business. What do I mean by that?

Some businesses just make money because it is their industry standard. Some businesses have a higher profit margin due to the nature of their business. They have less overhead (with the exception of payroll), and their pricing model depends on their reputation and marketability of the particular firm. A good example of this would be a personal service business.

It is much more difficult with other types of businesses. For example, the restaurant industry is not as profitable as it might seem. I personally had many clients who lost a lot of money in the restaurant business. You definitely need to know what you are doing and have at least a few years of experience before diving into that industry.

Unfortunately, quite often, when people decide to start their own businesses, the last person they want to run their ideas by are their CPAs. They might schedule visits with their attorneys for creating agreements and contracts, but CPAs usually learn about the business venture after the business has already started. It can be too late at this point. You might have a great idea, and even cash to sustain your business for a couple of months, but without a valid and realistic business model, you can go broke very shortly after you open your business. I believe that people don't want to see their accountants beforehand because they are afraid the CPA will start criticizing their business model. Accountants, in general, do tend to have a reputation of leaning more towards the pessimistic side of business. Unlike the

"Do not under-estimate getting a realistic second look from an accountant."

norm, I am a very enthusiastic accountant. However, when I see that numbers don't add up, I don't refrain from informing my clients of what I'm thinking. It's great to be optimistic about your business, but do not underestimate getting a realistic second look from an accountant.

Therefore, before you decide to buy a business or start your own from scratch, talk to an accountant! Another really important thing you must do is listen to your intuition. One of my clients shared her intuition story with me. Her intuition was telling her to stop investing into her new business when she reached $10,000. She did not listen to her own intuition and ended up losing at least fifteen times more in both time and money.

When you don't have experience in a particular industry, take the time to learn more about it before you invest your money in it. Talk to your CPAs, business coaches, and advisors, and get their opinions about the business model. Learn from their experiences, but most importantly make sure you love the type of business you are taking part in. If you do something just for the money, then you are more likely to be willing to give up on it later.

Once you pass this test and start your business, there are weekly activities that you must do to make sure your business can sustain financially.

Implementing Daily, Monthly and Quarterly Accounting Activities to Move Your Business Forward

Complete your finances in a timely manner, reconcile your accounts and know your business numbers. You cannot make intelligent decisions if you don't know your true numbers. Let's discuss items that would need your attention on a daily, weekly, monthly, quarterly, and annual basis.

Every day you should know your cash position in the bank. For example, I use my bank's iPhone app to access my bank account every morning and review transactions to ensure accuracy, cash flow purposes, collections, and planning. It allows me to catch fraudulent transactions, see who cleared checks, and

"Every day you should know your cash position in the bank."

plan for the next two weeks on what expenses should be paid immediately. This practice also prevents the embarrassment that comes with having uncleared checks and negative balance account charges.

Additionally, every week my team and I have a team meeting where we review our scorecards and weekly performances (this includes my own). We also discuss our production and projects for the week as well as assign billings. Then on that same day, my assistant bills our clients and sends reminders regarding outstanding invoices. I pull the Accounts Receivable Aging report to see what actions need to be taken to collect on older accounts. We believe that cash collections should be a very intentional process that is never put aside. It is a well-known fact that the longer a bill stays outstanding, the less chances it will be paid during collections. We will cover the Accounts Receivable Aging report more in Chapter 4.

We also pay our vendors every Friday and sometimes even prepay up to three months in advance to ensure our office services won't be disrupted. Paying smaller bills in advance will not drastically affect your cash flow, and it will save you money and time on writing these smaller checks every month. Some of our bills are withdrawn electronically (which would be another reason to check your cash position daily in your bank). Cash collection reports, billings, and bills are taken care of on a weekly basis. As you can see, billings require the most frequent attention to manage cash efficiently. Cash is king! You can have income but go broke by the time you collect it! Always stay intentional about your collections process and procedures. Don't be shy to ask for your money in a timely manner—it is yours, you earned it!

Every month we complete our bank and credit card accounts reconciliation and review our financial reports. You should do these same activities to ensure you have visibility of your financial standing, as it is a key to building a successful business and high net worth. Remember the saying, "Whatever you focus on multiplies?" The same is true here. To build an intentionally successful business you need to get in the habit of reviewing your financial data weekly or even daily (at least some parts of your reports), and compare it with forecasted figures and your monthly budget. This information also serves you and your accountant in vital tax planning activities. If you are not comfortable with bank reconciliation or accounting in general, please hire an accounting professional to oversee your accounting and reconciliation needs. Don't think about saving money by doing it yourself, as this could cost you much more in the long run when the accountants have to go back and fix your mistakes. In our firm, we offer monthly all-inclusive packages that assist entrepreneurs in their business decision-making process and tax planning, as well as compliance issues. If you need the same type of service, feel free to contact us. We would love to help you to be more successful!

Accounting Tools: QuickBooks

Nowadays, you or your accountant should utilize software with real time data-sharing capabilities to give you added visibility of your financial standing. That means you can utilize either QuickBooks Online (QBO) or the regular desktop QuickBooks software that can be shared between you and your clients with a cloud hosting solution, such as Right Networks.

Either QBO or desktop QuickBooks software with cloud-hosting implementation can be a great solution for those seeking professional accounting services. This software streamlines communication with your accountant so that you can easily share your numbers with him or her and access your business reports anytime, anywhere Internet is available. These software programs also provide paperless solutions for your receipts, billings and other activities. Paperless helps keep records organized and secure while being kind to the environment. Also, you don't need to worry about your computer crashing; leave it to the big guys to handle your security. In our office, we use desktop QuickBooks with the hosting component of a third party provider to allow us and our clients shared access to their business books.

What and how can this be done? If you are new to QuickBooks, your initial goal should be to set up either QBO or any other online accounting software. Several options are available, such as Xero, Sage, Freshbooks, and many more. Once your company is set up in QBO, it is time to connect your business checking accounts to your QB software. Make sure that you connect business accounts only! It is a very easy and straightforward process. I still recommend your accountant or bookkeeper do it on your behalf as she/he will set up your accounts properly and allocate your expenses from these accounts to the correct number in the chart of accounts.

Once you get set up correctly in the accounting software for the very first time, the system will remember most of the activities and to which account they should be allocated. That way, the next time a similar expense shows up in QB or QBO, the system will automatically suggest the account where it needs to be posted. Since the majority of business expenses are repeating every month, you only really need to set up the transaction rules the first time a transaction comes up. After that, every time a similar or identical transaction comes up, the system will automatically remember it and classify it for you. Once you create a proper set up in QBO or QB, the majority of the work

"Invest in learning technology at the beginning and then it will work correctly by saving you time, money, and energy."

is complete. Remember, nowadays, technology is your friend! Invest in learning technology at the beginning and then it will work correctly by saving you time, money, and energy.

If you meet a bookkeeper who wants to keep a QB copy on her computer and send you a report every month for you to review and reconcile for your company, then I recommend to run away! Not seeing your reports in a timely manner or not being able to access the QB file is the worst for your business's financial health. Don't hold your business data hostage, leaving it to depend on just one person. In my practice, I have seen many clients whose accountants passed away or disappeared (one even went to jail for embezzlement). This leaves some very frustrated business owners behind. These business owners could not retrieve data and ended up paying significant penalties to the IRS or other professionals to recreate all of the data again! This is especially true for payroll records. When the government system allows to accept electronic reports, file it electronically. Make sure you keep electronic backup and have proof that all records were indexed timely and submitted to tax agencies. Utilizing new software solutions for your business, and connecting them to your apps, smart phone, etc., is the only way to go in this modern age.

Then you should review your budgeted and forecasted items with your actual numbers on a quarterly basis. Why do I say review both? Because budgeted items can prevent overspending. Budgeting helps you figure out why more expenses occurred and how to correct them. The forecasted amounts help you see your projected revenues and what actions need to be taken to increase them. Are you on track to achieve your goals? Remember that you must find a balance in management of expenses, implementing strategies and accountability for revenue growth.

We also do employee reviews on a semi-annual basis because performance is directly tied to our income and expense numbers. What other non-financial key performance indicators are essential for your growth and revenue reductions? Review and discuss these items with your leadership team.

Again, scorecards are our friends! Please refer to *Table 7* in the Appendix for a sample of Key Performance Indicators (KPIs). We set goals for each team member in terms of production and billings. At my firm, this is the difference between administrative time and billable time as well as how much of that billable time spent was actually billed to the client. These indicators help us figure out whether we are making money on each client, whether our employees are efficient, and whether the price for our services was set correctly. We utilize value billing, which means that the price for our services is communicated upfront and not billed hourly. We still track the number of hours spent per client on a project to help determine if we provided the right quote or undercharged the client for future reference. When setting indicators for employees, however, make sure to set expectations accordingly. For example, an experienced accountant will require less time to finish a project, so their goals will be different than those of someone who is just starting out in the company. People most likely will not be as efficient as they will be one year from now, so always keep that in mind. This is also true when the company is in high growth mode. High growth mode is the time when lots of new clients are added to the firm. This may also take additional time to set up new clients, especially if you are just getting to know the client. Taking these factors into consideration will establish proper expectations when planning for productivity and cash flow.

Action Items:

1. Hire a trusted accounting professional to do your monthly compliance work as well as be your advisor and fractional CFO to provide you with full interpretation of your business financials and help you with proactive tax and financial planning.

2. Utilize software such as QB or QBO for creation of financial statements. No excel spreadsheet can provide you with complete, double entry accounting data!

3. Reconcile your business bank accounts and review your business reports on a monthly basis.

4. Invite and add your accountant to your QB software, so he or she will have an instant access to your data, should you have any questions.

   It is also a great tool for tax planning and tax preparation purposes as I assume you will not be preparing your tax returns by yourself.

5. Review your financial reports with your accountant and management team.

6. Review your forecasts and budgets with your management team.

7. Review your employee performance on a quarterly basis, as well as other non-financial KPIs (Key Performance Indicators).

Selecting Key Performance Indicators to Predict Future Business Performance

KPIs or Key Performance Indicators are essential factors for business growth and development. They help you create business forecasts as well as evaluate current performance. The ability to determine critical key performance indicators for your business will allow you to create a scorecard and measure your business direction on a consistent basis. At our firm we use scorecards on a weekly basis and discuss our performance during our weekly meetings. Scorecards help us see our performance and compare it with other team members, our forecasted goals and previous periods. What can be measured can be improved. It works! I strongly

"What can be measured can be improved."

suggest that every business with employees and systems should implement scorecards into their business metrics. In order to create accountability tools, such as scorecards, you first need to determine what essential key performance indicators determine your business. Just by reviewing a few of them, you can see trends and be able to predict the future direction of your business.

Let's determine a few key performance indicators that play an important role in your business. Let's break them into several categories such as revenue, growth, net income, productivity, employee efficiency, cash flow management, debt management and customer and employee satisfaction. Personal service businesses are not heavily invested in machinery and equipment, but if your industry requires significant investments in particular fixed assets, measuring the efficiency (return on fixed assets) is also very important.

1. **Revenue Growth Rate**

   Your Revenue Growth Rate is a critical indicator of your business's health. Revenue is your gross revenue over a given period. While having a positive revenue is undoubtedly a positive sign, revenue alone does not give you an accurate snapshot of your business's health. You want to ensure that your revenue is growing over time. A positively trending revenue will signal new opportunities and is essential for long-term decision making as it allows you to measure the extent to which your business is growing.

   Revenue Growth Rate = [(Revenue for this current period
   (make sure same time periods are taken into calculation)
   – revenue from previous year) /
   revenue from the previous period]*100%

   For example, if your gross business revenue last year was $200,000 and this year it is $300,000 then:

   $300,000 – $200,000 = $100,000 growth

[$100,000 / $200,000] *100 = 50%.
This means that your business grew by 50%!

When you start your business from $0 revenue, you can easily grow it by 100% or even 300%. I remember when I started my practice I was excited sharing my revenue numbers. We grew 50%! You can double your revenue very fast at first. This is especially feasible when you operate your business under capacity, meaning you have more time to do the work but not enough work.

As your business grows, you'll see that your actual revenue and growth percentage will start to go down because 100% growth from $300,000 is another $300,000. Gain understanding that your % of revenue growth will be growing at a decreasing rate, unless something drastic changes in your company to allow handling aggressive and fast growth.

Now that you know this, make sure that you don't over-extend yourself! It's tempting to put all your efforts in marketing and growth, but if you don't have systems in place or trained people, it can become twice as much work for you! Very often, aggressive growth can cause businesses to suffer or even go out of business due to lack of resources to sustain that aggressive growth. If you keep up with recent tabloids, you might remember the effect Kate Middleton's engagement brought to a company called Issa. Kate Middleton was wearing Issa's dress when they announced her engagement to Prince William. The company became so popular that within 5 minutes all of the dresses were sold out on the company website because too many orders were placed. The company did not have the resources to support all of those orders and had to bring another partner to help out. This addition to the team caused great turbulence within the company and was potentially one of the main reasons the company split later. Imagine if you stretch your marketing resources, and lots of people want to call your company to place orders, except you don't have enough people to deliver services in a timely and quality manner. In my opinion, doubling your growth in year one, 50% in year two, and 30% growth every year after that is a sustainable goal for your business that will lead to steady and healthy growth.

When your growth declines, or your sales decline, always compare specific periods and look for an explanation as to why that might be happening. Is your business gaining a bad reputation? Perhaps someone on your team does not service your customers in a professional manner. Did a competitor move next to your business location? Try to analyze the reasons behind this decline in sales so that you may take corrective action as soon as you can. Don't procrastinate and hope that things will turn around quickly! Instead you can be proactive and hire a professional to analyze it with you. This is why the weekly scorecards come in very handy, as you can catch the problem almost immediately.

2. **Net Income Ratio**

Your Net Income Ratio (also called Net Profit Percentage), measures your business's efficiency over time by revealing profits after you have paid taxes and all costs of production. You can determine this ratio by dividing your net profits by net sales and multiplying by 100 to formulate a percentage. Your net income ratio should be performed on a monthly basis. Compare your month-to-month net income ratio to better understand the health of your organization.

$$\text{Net Profit} = \text{Revenue} - \text{Expenses}$$

$$\text{Net Sales} = \text{Sales} - (\text{Cost of Sales Returns} + \text{Allowances} + \text{Discounts})$$

$$\text{Net Income Ratio} = (\text{Net Profit} / \text{Net Sales}) \times 100$$

You need to know these industry specific ratios to compare your business with others. Service based businesses should have at least 10-15% net income ratio. Some business owners see their net income ratios at 30-40% and should pat themselves on the back since those are hard numbers to reach. It is still recommended to your CPA review your numbers as the income/expenses numbers can be skewed.

For example, being an owner of an S-corporation allows you to pay yourself a reasonable salary and deduct it as a business expense from your company. You take the rest of the money as shareholder's distributions, which do not decrease your income, as distributions are an equity account. For example, let's say you had an income of $80,000 for the past year. You take $20,000 as a salary and $60,000 as distributions, thus leaving $60,000 as net income in your business. It can be a good number and your net income ratio can be quite high. However, it might not represent your "true" income if, let's say, you wanted to bring in a manager to replace you. What would be the fair market salary of the manager? I doubt it would be the $20,000 you are choosing to pay yourself. You will most likely need to pay the full $80,000. That could mean that your business will make no money.

3. **Productivity/Employee Efficiency**

Have you ever asked yourself questions such as, *how productive are my employees?* What do you do to calculate your employee efficiency? Do you have benchmarks to compare? In our CPA firm we use software that is specifically designed for tax and accounting firms, called Practice CS. It combines all information needed to run a successful firm. It securely stores a client's personal and contact information on the cloud, and helps keep track of the projects each team member is currently working on and/or finished with. This helps track the number of billable hours an employee spent on a client, leaving you to make the decision of how much you want to charge the client. As I already mentioned, we use value billing, meaning we tell you your price upfront. Our clients know how much our services will cost them. However, we still keep track of our time worked on a particular project. This helps me know how much time was spent by each employee on each client and what the reason was if we went over the budget. This information helps us to predict next year and take corrective action if needed.

How does your company keep track of your team members' productivity? If you have not done so yet, start researching software that supports your industry. Learn it well and have all team members use it.

"How does your company keep track of your team members' productivity?"

Set up benchmarks, a break-even analysis, and implement scorecards so that you can keep track on a weekly basis where you and your employees stand. Are they profitable? Do they make you money? Do they make you lose money with their lack of productivity, lack of training and experience? What can you do to help your team members to succeed?

Come up with your individual Key Performance Indicators (KPIs) to be able to tell the employee's performance. Can't place your finger on what is to blame for rising costs and depleted profits? Often, it is your inability to effectively produce your goods or services—whether it stems from ineffective equipment, processes, or even your employees. Run productivity KPIs regularly. These KPIs should be predetermined and tailored to specific job functions. Conduct quarterly performance reviews to determine if employees met KPIs effectively. Invest in your employees regularly. Try to determine what tasks they are good at naturally and use those natural talents to your advantage. By investing in their continued education, allowing them to attend seminars, and most importantly training them in the company's processes, you will help them become most profitable for your business.

4. **Cash Flow**

Cash provides a vital safety net for your business. It's the most liquid asset and can pull you out of a tight spot in a moment's notice. Conduct the operating cash flow ratio to determine how much cash your business generates and spends over a given period of time. If there is too little cash at-hand, it could signal your business has some underlying problems (even if your revenue or net income is strong). Your revenue and net income can be strong if you review your reports on accrual basis. Under accrual method of accounting, you see your revenue when you create invoices for your customers and when you enter invoices from your vendors. However, your reports under cash method of accounting can tell you a totally different story if your customers have not paid you yet! To determine cash flow, you must compute various formulas to better understand the ins and outs of your cash.

The operating cash flow ration is a measure of how well you can cover your current liabilities. Operating cash flow ratio = cash flow from operations (can be found in operating cash flow section of your cash flow report) divided by current liabilities. If the ratio is more than 1, that means you will be able to meet your short term cash obligations.

To avoid cash flow shortages, make sure to have at least two to three months' reserves to cover business operating expenses. I know it can be a lot, especially when businesses are in the growth state. Growth takes all the cash! At this time, you could also work on your availability of getting external funding such as credit cards, or lines of credits. It never hurts to be safe in case of a cash emergency!

5. **Debt Measurement**

Measure how effectively you're using business funds by measuring debt. Calculate credit and other liabilities and divide by your total equity. This formula is known as a debt-to-equity ratio.

Debt-to-Equity Ratio = Liability / Shareholder's Equity

(Keep in mind that the smaller the answer,
the healthier the company!)

6. **Return on fixed assets**

Was your latest capital investment worth it? This formula
is key in determining just how lucrative a fixed-assets
investment might be. The fixed asset turnover formula
evaluates how effectively fixed assets (furniture, machinery, equipment) was allocated and can show its role in
net sales. A higher ratio indicates a positive outcome. Of
course, some industries must invest heavily in equipment
and it can take a few years before they are able to recapture these expenses. Again, before you invest, discuss it
with your CPA to make sure the spending makes sense
and no other alternative solutions are available.

7. **Customer and Employee Satisfaction**

Customer and employee satisfaction is one of the most vital
and multi-faceted KPIs for businesses. You can measure
satisfaction by conducting annual surveys. Ensure surveys
are quantifiable by using a numbered grading scale. For
example, ask respondents to fill out a 5 if they're highly
satisfied or a 1 if they are highly dissatisfied with your
products/services. Surveys should be conducted regularly
and compared over time to detect trends.

During our weekly meetings at the firm, we discuss the number of complaints and the number of lost clients in our scorecards. If we lose a client because of our actions, we discuss in greater detail what went wrong and make sure all lessons are learned so that the mistake is not repeated in the future.

Have you checked your business reviews online lately? If not, please do so as online presence and prestige is becoming more and more crucial to the business world with each passing day. We recommend to reach out to your best clients—your very satisfied customers—and ask them to post their reviews online. This strategy could help motivate clients to trust your firm more.

Comparing Your Financials with Last Year's Records

After you've established KPIs and your financial data are assembled and completed, compare financial reports (as well as non-financial items within your business) with those recorded in the previous year. Your comparisons will help you better understand your business strengths, weakness, and the current progress towards your financial goals. They will also aid in spotting errors or overlooked assets and liabilities that could have massive ramifications on your financial reports.

Comparing income statements will enable you to see how much of your gross revenue, expenses, and net income have changed compared to last year. You will gain understanding of what changed and why. An income statement report shows business revenue and expenses for a particular period of time. For example, January 1st to December 31st. You can also generate a comparison report and compare your income and expenses for two years. QuickBooks software allows you to select an option that does a comparison percentage to your gross sales, so that you can see how much of each item is affected. For example, how much of your net income can be compared to gross revenue. If you are confused, initially, I would suggest that you hire an accountant to go over your reports and learn how to generate them.

Now, let's discuss balance sheet items and reports. Your business's balance sheet shows a "snapshot" of your assets, liabilities, and shareholder equity at a certain point in time. Let's use December 31, 2019 as an example. The balance sheet is an itemized list that is structured around the basic accounting equation: Assets = Liabilities + Shareholder Equity. A balance sheet report shows your business assets, liabilities, and its net worth (retained earnings). The assets part shows you what your business has in its possession at the time. This can be something such as furniture, equipment, security deposits, accounts receivable (how much customers owe you), investments, etc. The liabilities section shows you how much your business owes to other people (vendors). This can be debts such as credit cards, loans, lines of credit, payroll taxes, and other current (payment is due within one year) or long-term (payment is due longer than one year) liabilities. Comparing balance sheet items, such as an increase of cash in the bank and undeposited funds, an increase or decrease of accounts receivable, reduction of debt, or an increase in fixed assets are typically good indicators that the business is growing and more investments were made to take it to the next level. Each balance sheet account and its change can tell you the story of your business and its future direction.

Obviously, if your debt is increasing, something is wrong. Unless you can see that fixed assets are increasing as well (which might just mean that you had to make a temporary sacrifice for long-term profits). Pay attention to your shareholder's distributions or partner draws (if your business operates as a partnership), and to how much money is withdrawn from the business.

These two financial reports serve different purposes and each offers a unique perspective on the health of your business. This is why working with a CFO and CPA can be very beneficial. They can interpret your statements and suggest improvements to your company for you.

Your income statement, also called your Profit and Loss (P&L) statement, shows the profitability of your business over time. It evaluates your revenue, income and expenses.

By gaining visibility of both your income statement and balance sheet items, you'll be able to identify trends and your business's worth. To get an accurate understanding of developing trends, compare at least three years of financial reports. This will help you understand what items are vital to long-term growth and what aspects may have been anomalies.

Examining Your Non-Financial Assets

When you start your business, it is easy to become disappointed when your numbers on the income statements do not correspond with your expectations. However, the financial side of the business is only one side. You need to review your non-financial assets, such as the experiences you are gaining by performing a particular type of work, the business connections you are making, as well as the reputation you are building for your business. People, experiences, expertise, better office or store location, company culture, great new clients, better vision and direction for your company, better business connections, and new opportunities are some of the non-financial items you'll want to include in your valuation. Please use *Tables 2* and *3* in the Appendix to review your business financial and non-financial assets. Note the Fair Market Value (FMV) and its effect on the company's long-term success. This is why when businesses are sold, the reputation, systems, team members, efficient operations, and other secret recipes are not on your balance sheet. However, when you sell your business and the price difference between the sales price and the fixed assets on your balance sheet becomes goodwill (what are otherwise known as non-financial assets). This will become a very valuable intangible asset and can turn into a financial asset. Therefore, never underestimate the value of your non-financial assets. One day they might make you a fortune!

"Never underestimate the value of your non-financial assets. One day they might make you a fortune!"

Stay positive, even through the hard times of your business development stages. Keep going and get yourself a great support team. Examining your non-financial assets can have a powerful effect on your net worth.

Your non-financial items are the backbone to your financial success.

→ Action Items:

1. **Run comparison reports in your QuickBooks software.** Compare last year's numbers with this year's numbers by category, including revenues, expenses, and cash in the bank, accounts receivable amounts, fixed assets, and debt items.

2. **Explore causal relationships on your own or meet with a CPA or a financial advisor who can help translate financial patterns, so that you can better understand what numbers to change.** Your financial advisor should be able to address your financial concerns and offer corrective actions to discourage poor financial performance.

3. **Make a list of your last year success.**
   List all your non-financial achievements you are proud of. Did you get a great team member? How did you do it or what did you do differently this time? Analyze your systems for better decision making.

---

4. **Place a value for your non-financial assets.**
    How do you think it helped or will help your business
    in the future? Even non-financial assets have a sig-
    nificant financial value, perhaps not immediately, but
    in the future for sure. (Use the non-financial value
    sheet in the Appendix as a guide).

Creating Your Cash Flow Statements and Examining Your Cash Availability for Growth

You might already be aware that business growth uses a lot of cash. Cash is needed to cover operating expenses, to invest into the company's infrastructure (ex. machinery and equipment), and to pay employees who might not work at 100% capacity yet, due to business growth, and/or might not be efficient enough due to having a new job. As the saying goes, "hire for not where you are but where you want to be." Therefore, growth will require cash! Your business might be profitable according to your income statements, but very close to bankruptcy in terms of cash flow. Cash flow management and improvements consist of many techniques, including accounts receivable timely billings and collections, implementation of prepayments or retainers, billing customers in arrears (as you go), following through on collection procedures, watching for expenses, and many more.

Many factors can influence the bottom line and cash collec-tions for the business. For example, let's examine revenue increase vs. price increase, as well as volume or number of customers served, obtaining additional source of income and implementing other highly leveraged ways to generate additional revenue, decrease of operating and direct expenses, and cash collection procedures.

I also suggest that you create a business forecast along with scorecards implementation to be able to predict your future outcome of cash movements in your business, your gross sales, your net income and other cash inflow and outflow expected activities.

▶ **Action items:**

1. **Run your cash flow reports every month to get your-self familiar with cash movements.** Run an Accounts Receivable aging report every week or twice per month to see how much customers owe you and how many days past due their invoices are. At our firm, we check our bank balance daily and run aging accounts receivable reports every week before our team meeting.

2. **Create collections procedures and implement them on a consistent basis.** Remember newer debt is much easier to collect than the older debt. The longer your debt is outstanding, the harder it is to collect. Stay on top of your customer's collections.

3. **Hire someone on a part-time commission basis to collect your accounts receivable.** Think and implement ideas on how to keep the leverage to protect your cash collections in full and in a timely manner.

4. Create a forecast and budget to be able to predict your future cash collection, your expenses and prevent huge fluctuations between high and low cash collections.

5. **Change your billing strategy.** For example, at our CPA office, we are big proponents of providing services that are offered as a monthly package. It creates a much better cash flow for us, clients are happy because they know what is included in the services (pretty much everything) and their cash outflow is also predictable in terms of amount and timing. There are no surprises, and every transaction is consistent and predictable.

CHAPTER **4**

Forecasting and Budgeting

IT IS important to compare finances with the budgeted amounts established at the beginning of the year. When accountants work with business owners, we analyze historical data most of the time. Sometimes we can make corrective actions going forward, but this isn't always the case. This is why budgeting and forecasting play an important role in your business (which may rollover to your personal life as well). Let's discuss the main reasons why budgeting and forecasting are important and what the difference between them is.

Budgeting is mainly focused on where business owners want to go. Business owners predict revenue and expenses based on the previous year numbers. As you might know, it is used in non-profits and governmental agencies as a form of permission to spend the budgeted money. If a big corporation has a precise amount of budgeted marketing or charitable amount, then chances are that they will most likely spend that budgeted amount of money before the end of the year. Also, people are encouraged to spend

"A budget is focused on distributions of expenses. It has very little impact on income."

the money before the year end so that they will be given the same or more next year. A budget is focused on predictions on how the business will operate, how much income will be generated and gives more precise number on expenses.

Forecasting, on the other hand focuses mainly on income and cash flow movements. First of all, it can preside your cash flow. We cannot say for sure what the cash inflow will be, unless we are meeting our target in sales projections, but we can tell what the cash outflow will be with more accuracy. That helps us to predict and avoid some cash flow issues.

A budget can help with tax planning and owners' distributions. When you see where you are planning to be financially three months from now for example, you can predict how much payroll you need to make as well as distributions for yourself.

As you become more intentional about your spending, savings, and investments, you will also decrease your chances of getting into debt, and you will have a better chance of paying your existing debt faster. Budgeting also helps you with planning for the purchasing of assets as well as hiring.

All equipment and other investment options should be planned at the beginning of the year. Review, reflect and see what caused significant discrepancies and how they can be better planned for in the future. Plan for emergencies by establishing savings accounts and taking distributions at the end of the year. After all of your tax planning is complete, you can feel empowered knowing that your cash flow will increase thanks to your due diligent work.

"When you add intention to any of the aspects of your life...you get significantly better results."

Overall, budgeting creates an intention around managing money. When you add intention to any of the aspects of your life, including the building of your business, hiring the right people for your team, select clients and customers you want to work with, as well as the way you manage your money, you get significantly better results.

Practice Budgeting to become even more successful!

Action Items:

1. Create a budget per month using QB software, Excel spreadsheet or any other software.

2. Compare your budgeted and actual amounts on a monthly basis and go over the discrepancies as to why there could be differences.

3. Once identified, develop an action plan to address these differences. This will help you avoid future

discrepancies and provide a clearer picture of your finances in the future.

4. Prepare your budget for the next year using the insights you've just developed.

5. Review current and historic budgets to identify trends.

6. Establish an emergency fund in your budget that can be used for unexpected business or personal expenses.

Forecasting of Cash Inflow: How to Double Your Income This Year

In whatever we do, sales and marketing are the most important tasks for small business owners, just like for everyone else. Marketing is prevalent in all areas of our lives; for example, you need to market yourself to a future employer, to a prestigious college, or even to a potential marriage partner. There is no doubt that marketing is essential for growing your business. Let's combine the ideas of forecasting, budgeting, and marketing in order to significantly increase your income this year.

"Forecasts are built on faith, hope, and desire, versus budgeting being built on fear of running out of money."

Creating a business forecast is more exciting than creating budgets because, in my opinion, forecasts are built on faith, hope, and desire, versus budgeting being built on fear of running out of money.

So, let's dream big and create a plan on how we can get there. Step number one should be to review your last year's numbers and predict your business growth. For example, let's say your last year's gross revenue number was $250,000 and you want it to be $400,000 this year. It is a stretch goal in my opinion, as it is 60% in growth projection. This is considered a stretch because, as you might remember, we talked about how having a 30% growth every year is a healthy number.

First of all, determine why you chose this number for growth. Does this number only reflect the minimum you need to make a comfortable living with your new predictable net income? Is it the number of your ideal goals? Or is there another reason why this is the number you chose?

Second, determine if your business can sustain the 60% growth. Do you have enough resources to deliver your products or services worth your projected revenue?

When I decided on the right number for my business to grow, I predicted aggressive growth and prepared for it by hiring new team members and training them. We also moved to a new, bigger, more comfortable office. We were ready! I felt that I needed this growth because my last year gross revenue became my expenses this year. That means that if I didn't choose to grow, I would have personally made no money this year or the company would have no net income. I had no options but to grow my business.

After I determined that all the numbers make sense and I had enough to support our resources, we needed to create and consistently apply our system on growth strategy.

New money can be generated via current or new clients. Let's talk about ways of generating revenue from your current customers.

First of all, let's examine what worked in the past and how you got more business from current customers. Were there referrals from current customers? Did you add additional services or products to your clients such as insurance, additional coaching sessions, etc.? Did you start offering package deals for repeat business transactions? Did you change your billing policy and start charging monthly verses annually, thus increasing cash inflow? Or did you simply increase the prices for your customers?

Sometimes this technique in itself can generate up to an additional 5% or more in revenue growth. In fact, my firm has increased prices in the past year due to the increased volume of work we were performing for some clients (which shows their businesses are growing too!) as well as our internal evaluation of expenses and overhead costs. Do not be discouraged

"Always have trust in yourself, your self-worth and your business's potential!"

and afraid to make price changes as hesitation will not serve you in the future. Never make any business decisions based on fear! It is a short-term emotion and it will never serve you nor your business! Always have trust in yourself, your self-worth and your business's potential!

For step number two, let's start by brainstorming your ideas, creating a plan and a setting up a system on how you can bring more revenue over a specified time period with predictable outcome.

There are so many revenue-generating ideas available, particularly social media. The secret is not to get overwhelmed and spread yourself so thin that none of the ideas will be implemented.

Ask yourself this question: What worked in the past for your business? What did not only bring you clients but also brought you joy doing it?

For example, I have always enjoyed presenting in front of fellow business owners. It has inadvertently also worked for me in terms of generating more business. I noticed that people who come to my seminars and presentations just to learn about taxes and equip themselves with seemingly free information, most often ended up being my clients afterwards! Most likely they did not have an accountant on their current team of professionals, and after learning more about taxes, they felt even more overwhelmed than before. This led to me being hired on the spot once or twice! Public speaking is my forte, but you need to find what your strength is and focus on it. What has worked for you in the past? If giving presentations have worked for you, for example, then do them more often!

Have you joined any networking groups? I was part of the BNI® (Business Network International) for almost ten years. I just left this group as I want to take more time to travel. However, I can confidently state that BNI® is responsible for at least 25% of my company's gross revenue overall. This is a significant amount and it goes to show the quality of people that are part of that business group. Have you ever considered being a member of any networking organization? It could be the decision that helps bring in that extra revenue! If socializing is not your preferred method then try finding other strengths.

For me personally, one of my strengths comes from something as simple as my background. I came from Russia over 21 years ago and Russian is and will always be my first language. This really helped me find my niche set of clients when I first started. I decided to advertise my CPA services in the Russian community of Denver, Colorado. I would say that to this day, half of our clients are Russian-speaking business owners who came from the former Soviet Union. The majority of them speak Russian and feel like they have a personal connection with my business. We even recently hired an additional Russian-speaking team member to help with the many Russian-speaking clients we have. This goes to show that finding your niche and getting into those communities can also be crucial to your business growth.

Are you using Social Media? We even get business from YouTube, Facebook as well as LinkedIn! Positive Google reviews were also very helpful and have generated us several clients in the past. I know one chiropractor in Denver who shared with me that he gets more than 30 customers per day just from direct Google searches! Now that's the power of the Internet!

Action Items:

1. Mastermind and create ways to generate revenue.

2. Create a system and follow it for at least several months.

3. Ask your current customers for more referrals by inviting them for coffee, lunch and just have meetings with them at least a handful of times a year.

4. Don't forget to send a thank you note with a gift card in it after you received a referral from any of your clients. I have had so many thank you notes sent my way just for sending thank you cards to my clients after referring clients to me. I believe this is a very good practice as people want to feel appreciated and will keep you and your business in mind more often!

5. Annually go over your client/customer base and see who needs to be "let go." (Pick clients that you constantly lose money on, who are difficult to work with, or the clients whose problems greatly outweigh the benefits of keeping them).

6. Always think about how you can increase value for your current clients.

7. Utilize sales forecasts.

If you follow your new marketing steps consistently, your business will grow fairly quickly. Just keep in mind that a consistent approach is the key!

Planning for Debt Repayment

As we already briefly discussed this topic in our "Increase Your Net Worth" section, I think it is worth repeating. If you have credit card debt or other outstanding installment accounts, plan for these repayments accordingly in your budget and cash flow analysis. You will not be taking a tax deduction for repayments, as these expenses were already calculated. Debt repayment is far from a cut and dry topic. As Dave Ramsey from Financial Peace University suggests, start repaying using the "debt snowball method" rather than the traditional method of debt repayment. While the traditional route of repayment involves paying off debts with

"Your emotions and psychological wellbeing profoundly impact your financial success."

the highest interest rate first, it is not always the right move. You may think it makes financial sense to pay off the highest interest rates first, but there's far more at play than just dollars and cents. Your emotions and psychological wellbeing profoundly impact your financial success. Ramsey's snowball method takes these psychological effects into consideration and consequently encourages you to pay off smaller loans in their entirety before paying off larger loans, regardless of interest rate. By paying off debts one at a time in their entirety, you are able to stay motivated as you wipe out one debt after the other.

To create a snowball method debt repayment plan you'll need to list all of your debts from the smallest to largest amounts. This growing repayment method should be meticulously planned for and you should know exactly when you need to finish paying each loan before you start. You should also calculate your anticipated income to ensure the projected payments fit your budget. Take added precautions by ensuring that at least two months of your business expenses can be covered with the available balance in your business checking account.

Action Items:

1. **Create a list of debts and put them in order from smallest to largest principals.** (You can also use unsecured debt in *Table 4* of the Appendix of this book.

2. **Go over your newly created debt list and note the repayment amount and time frame for repayment.** Calculate this timeframe based on your anticipated income.

3. **Analyze the reason why you incurred this debt in this first place.** Was it something unplanned? Was it during a period where your business was losing

money? Did you invest into something you could not afford? Review your reports to learn how to make better financial decisions in the future and avoid getting into debt in the first place.

4. **Remember, an excess of debt and its repayment will slow the business growth process!** So, be careful what you choose to utilize credit for when it comes to your business or personal expenses.

Reviewing Accounts Receivable Aging Summary Reports

Your Accounts Receivable, also known as Trade Receivables, is the money you are entitled to receive following a transaction between yourself and your customers. It is the amount of money your customers or clients owe you. Reviewing Accounts Receivable Aging Reports as well as having an effective cash collection practice in place can guarantee your financial wellness. Ideally, you should aim to have a business model that does not contain accounts receivable components, and purely handles cash transactions. Depending on your industry it might be possible or not.

Unfortunately, there is no such thing as all customers being ideal and paying on time. While some clients are amazing to work with, some customers might suddenly disappear once they receive the bill. This mad dash at the first sight of an invoice is a harsh reality of the business world. It even has some rather scary statistics to back it up. The longer an invoice goes unpaid, the less likely it is that you will ever receive payment. The Maryland Bar Association reports:

> ". . . An invoice over 60 days old has only a 70% chance of being collected in full. After 90 days of no payment, the chance of collecting the invoice in full drops to 45%. Once you pass the 120-day mark, it falls to a measly 20%."

This phenomenon can be easily thwarted with a proactive eye on Aging Accounts Receivable Report.

Most accounting software is equipped to alert you about pending invoices that show signs of potential non-payment. This information is collected and reported using Accounts Receivable Aging Summary reports. You should dedicate time to review these reports and take appropriate actions to ensure repayment of these unpaid invoices.

Do you know how much money your clients/customers owe you and how many days the invoice has been outstanding? Your accounting software should provide insight into these vital questions, provided that customer invoices were created in a timely manner using the same accounting software. Start contacting your customers using appropriate recoupment methods. Your goal should be to collect payments as soon as the services have been rendered in full. Follow up with clients frequently to ensure a timely payment.

This critical business activity not only supports your financial success, but instills pride in your work and boosts your self-esteem. If you are proud of what you have accomplished, the last thing you would want is to have someone take your hard work for granted, much less flat-out steal it. Get the recognition you deserve by making timely payment a requirement for everyone who receives your products or services. In addition, see if you can implement a "No Accounts Receivable" policy in your business. This will mean that all payments to your business will be done during the time of service delivery.

CHAPTER 5

Client Relations and Sales Management

NOW THAT we've covered the importance of debt repayment, here are a few techniques that can help you to improve your repayment rates. These tactics for forging stronger client relationships and boosting profitability with strategic sales management will ultimately increase cash flow and net worth. Taking retainers or prepayments can also be a good strategy for your business. It might seem like a lot of work to implement, but the possibilities of not having unpaid invoices will be worth it.

Enacting Cash Collection Policies

Always bill clients promptly, right after the work is complete. Clients are still in a state of gratitude for the work you have done and fast collection is very probable at this time.

Have well-defined cash collection procedures in writing. Encourage your team members to get involved in billing processes by following these guidelines precisely. You may want to avoid calling your clients personally when seeking payment. Billing can get messy. Clients may feel comfortable enough to give you all kinds of excuses why you will not get paid at that moment. Don't let the rapport you worked so hard to build with your clients get turned against you. Recognize the high-pressure tactics clients use and stay on alert for signs of aggression. Aggressive outburst may be likely, especially if they're already behind on payments. Instead, pull the old "good cop, bad cop" card and hire a collection professional adept at conflict resolution. By hiring a dedicated individual for such a role, your business demonstrates professionalism and helps ensure there are no hard feelings attached to the process.

Using Communication Best Practices

Implement a retainer policy that allows clients to make pre-payments for services. Have clear communication tools, such as service contract or written engagement letters. You may want to implement a Customer Relationship Management (CRM) platform to document customer communications and automate bill pay and other communication processes. These systems provide in-depth analysis of the effectiveness of your communication practices and how clients interact with these communications and marketing materials.

Obtain signed ACH forms from the client, when possible. This form states that a client has given you authorization to charge his or her business bank account on a certain day of the service completion. This is a great tool for clients when services are performed on a monthly basis as it ensures timely recurring payments.

Ask your business attorney to send collection letters if clients refuse to pay. This communicates to all parties involved that you take pride in your business and are serious about your services and self-worth. Typically, once legal professionals get involved, clients will be more persuaded to make a payment. However, use this as a last resort as it can be expensive and detrimental to business relationships.

Remind your clients of the kind of value you bring to the table. Take pride in your work and send your clients materials that add value to their businesses. Continue to build your relationship with clients through engaging, thoughtful actions. Perhaps you can go above and beyond the standard client-provider relationship by taking an unconventional approach that will brighten their day, like inviting them to events or special outings. These relationship-building tools help ensure timely payment and

> *"Remind your clients of the kind of value you bring to the table."*

give you a better understanding of your client and their values. This unique insight will ultimately help you deliver a more tailored product to your clients that help them achieve both their and your own goals.

Remain consistent in invoicing and client communication — no matter how difficult a particular client may be.

Being a business owner not only requires a cash inflow procedure, but a cash outflow procedure as well. We want to make sure to not get in trouble with the IRS and ensure that all of our tax deductions are deductible indeed. Based on my experience as a CPA, I have witnessed my clients getting in trouble for not issuing 1099 forms to their subcontractors or with the IRS disallowing some of their tax deductions. This is why I would like to address these issues in this chapter.

Reporting Payments to Independent Contractors

Independent contractors are one of those great non-financial assets that can help propel your success, but they come with some rather tricky financial strings that all businesses should be aware of. Unlike an employee, the employer is not responsible for withholding taxes from an independent contractor. Instead, independent contractors are paid in-full and often have to pay a lump sum of taxes at the end of the year. Before we discuss the compliance reporting issue for independent subcontractors, we need to discuss who would be considered as an independent subcontractor. The status of independent subcontractor or employee is not chosen by your subcontractor or you. There are certain IRS and State rules that determine whether a person can be classified as an independent subcontractor or if he or she should indeed be placed on your payroll.

There are three main tests that must be met: behavioral control, financial control, and type of relationship. Let's discuss each of the factors in detail:

1. **Behavioral control.** Are you providing your subcontractor with very detailed instructions on how the job should be performed? What tools and other equipment are required to complete the assignment? Do you expect your subcontractor to perform work at specific hours of the day? Do they come to your office at all?

2. **Financial control.** How do you pay your subcontractor? Is it per project or hourly? Do you provide benefits, such as health insurance, retirement plan contributions, or expense reimbursements? Does the subcontractor send you invoices and bills you when the project is complete?

3. **Type of relationship.** Do you have an agreement in writing? Did this subcontractor perform the same dues to other companies or offers services in the same capacity to others? Do they have their own company, such as LLC or Corporation? If you are not sure whether the particular person you hired should be treated as an independent subcontractor or employee, fill out form SS-8 and send it to the IRS. State rules might be slightly different and usually stricter. Consult with a professional regarding your particular situation.

Once you have determined that the person you hired is indeed an independent subcontractor, ask him or her to provide you with form W-9, where they list their personal or business name, SSN or company's EIN, address and signature. Based on the information provided, you will be able to issue them a form 1099-MISC in January.

Special steps must be taken to ensure that your payments made to these individuals are accurately reflected on Form 1099-MISC. Issuance of the form is essential in case you ever get audited. The IRS will have no issues allowing you this tax deduction. You must report your non-employee compensation spending if the following four conditions are met:

1. You made the payment to someone who is not on your payroll.
2. You made the payment for services as part of a business agreement, and not for personal matters.
3. You made the payment to an individual, partnership, estate, or in some cases, a corporation.
4. You made payments to the payee of at least $600 during the year.

The IRS scrutinizes all 1099-MISC forms as they are one of the primary reasons for income reporting discrepancies. The 1099-MISC is easily compared against an individual's 1099-MISC income reported on his or her income tax return. If the amounts don't match, the IRS will send you a letter informing you that the information you used for the 1099-MISC form does not match their records. Do not ignore the letter from IRS. Ask your independent subcontractors to review the information they provided to you to ensure the 1099-MISC form is error-free.

Make sure to follow tax filing deadlines for issuing forms to avoid penalties. Also, provide a copy to your subcontractor in a timely manner. The 1099-MISC tax filing deadline is January 31.

→ Action Items:

1. **Make a list of all non-employees who will get paid $600 or more this year from your business.** These are your independent contractors. The best way would be to review your QB data and, if classified correctly, run subtotal reports per person.

2. **Collect completed W-9 forms from all of your independent contractors, preferably before you give them their last check of the year.**

3. **Issue 1099-MISC forms to everyone who provided you with a W-9 form.** Your 1099-MISC forms should be mailed to independent contractors in January so that they can use it to report their personal income tax.

4. **If you hired an attorney, it does not matter how much you paid that person or company.** Issue them a 1099-MISC either way.

CHAPTER 6

Retirement Planning

PART OF finding success is investing in yourself to ensure a comfortable future for yourself. This can be accomplished with dedicated retirement planning. Choosing how to contribute to your retirement can be difficult, so I have outlined some important considerations to make when assessing your retirement strategy. Retirement plan contributions will not only save you money on taxes (in most cases), but will also help you gain a habit of investing into your future via making contributions and generating earnings.

"Part of finding success is investing in yourself to ensure a comfortable future for yourself."

Retirement Planning for Business Owners

Many people might feel confused and overwhelmed when they are employers of others or self-employed individuals. People often ask, what types of retirement accounts should I open? How much can I contribute there? The answer would be: it depends. It depends on factors such as your age, your adjusted gross income, your W-2 wages (depending on what type of business entity you operate) as well as if you have employees or not.

SEP IRA. This plan is applicable for both self-employed individuals who report their income on Schedule C of their individual tax return, and S-corporation shareholders-employees, who pay themselves a reasonable salary. If you are self-employed (SE), and perhaps don't even have an official business yet, you can contribute money to a Simplified Employee Pension (SEP) plan. In fact, technically you don't make a contribution, your business does it for you. It is a purely a business tax deduction and there is no catch up contribution. The SEP contributions limit is 20% of your Schedule C net income up to $56,000. Keep in mind that if SEP contributions are made for self-employed individuals, the owners of the company, they also have to be made for employees. For example, if your business's gross revenue is $100,000 and the expenses are $40,000, the net income would be $60,000. You can contribute 20% of your $60,000 to retirement.

The calculation is the following:

Step 1. $60,000 * 92.35%

(you need to adjust your income for SEP calculation purposes by one half of your self-employment tax) = $55,410

Step 2. $55,410 * 7.65% = $4,239

(adjustment for half of self-employment tax)

Step 3. $60,000 – $4,239 = $55,761

Step 4. $55,761 * 20% = $11,152

That leaves you with $11,152 maximum in retirement contributions. Don't get overwhelmed, as tax software calculates the maximum contribution for you. The maximum amount contributed cannot exceed $56,000. Also, you have to contribute to the SEP before you file a tax return with extension. The good news is that you have time to contribute until you file your tax return, by April 15th or up to October 15th (if you file a tax return extension). Employer contributions are not required, borrowing from the plan is not permitted, and standard 10% penalties on early distribution and 6% of access contributions will apply. Again, SEP IRA can be an ideal for business that are just starting out and have no employees. Even though, you can establish some qualification thresholds for your employees to qualify for the plan for a couple of years, I would still recommend another plan, such as Simple IRA or 401K.

If you have no employees in your business, and your business is taxed as an S-corporation, you should issue yourself a W-2 from your business as a reasonable shareholder's compensation. In this case, your SEP contribution limit will be 25% of your wages subject to FICA taxes, reported on your W-2 form. The maximum contribution limit can be up to $56,000. That means that your

"There are many retirement plans available for small business owners."

maximum W-2 wages should be $293,000. In this case, by paying yourself $293,000 in wages, might not be a smart move to have an S-corporation and SEP plan, as it defeats the idea of saving money on payroll taxes. Perhaps, having a solo 401K would be a much better solution. We will discuss that next.

Solo 401K. This qualified, profit-sharing retirement plan was designed specifically for employers or the self-employed that have no full-time employees other than the business owner and their spouse. This is one of the best plans which allows you a maximum contribution without maximizing your salary for FICA purposes, unlike SEP IRA. The maximum contribution is $56,000. It is a combination of your 401K employee contributions with a maximum of $19,000 or $25,000 if you are over 50 years of age, plus 25% of your FICA wages. It is very similar to the 401K but it was created solely for businesses with no employees. For example, you can pay yourself a $60,000 salary and be able to contribute $19,000 (under 50 years of age employee contribution) plus 25% of 60,000 = $15,000 as company deferral. Your total contribution will be $34,000. You need to have $136,000 in wages, subject to self-employment tax, if you had a SEP IRA!

Thus, by implementing Solo 401K instead of SEP IRA, you saved $10,738 in self-employment taxes! These plans are very inexpensive to manage, unlike regular 401K.

Simple IRA. Employers with 100 or fewer employees can establish this plan. The deadline to open a Simple IRA account is October 1st, to be effective for that same year. This is a very good option if you have employees besides yourself and your spouse. Employees can contribute, as a tax deferred income, up to $13,000 (with an additional $3,000 in catch-up contributions if over 50 year of age) plus a pre-determined company match, usually 3% of wages (but can be reduced to as low as 1% in any two out of five years). Employers' contributions are required if the employees contributed to the funds. The qualified employee for Simple IRA contribution would have to earn at least $5,000 from employers in the previous two years and should reasonably expect to do the same in the current year. The maintenance of the account is very inexpensive compared to maintaining a 401K. If you are new in business and have employees, this would be a good option.

Be careful about withdrawing funds from the Simple IRA as the penalties are 10% or 25% if funds are withdrawn within two years of the date you first contributed to the plan. As if that wasn't enough, withdrawals from these accounts will be subject to income tax as well! There might be some exceptions, and this should be discussed with your CPA.

Simple IRAs allow easy set-up and maintenance. It allows the participant to choose how funds are invested as opposed to a plan administrator through the employer. Participants are always 100% vested in the plan from the beginning.

401K. This is an ideal plan when you make more significant contributions such as $19,000 or $25,000 (when 50 or older) and have profit sharing components. This plan can be discriminatory for key employees. Despite the fact that it is more expensive to maintain this plan, it provides a better tax savings opportunity by contributing more money into retirement accounts. Traditional 104K will cost about $1,000-$1,500 to administer as you would have to work with a plan administrator and asset manager. Do an extensive research of who do you want your plan with. When you use Paychex or ADP, they most likely sell you a 104K. I would not just to their plan options, due to high costs, and not so great customer service.

Another great feature of 401K is the ability to select a Roth IRA component. Again, consult with your CPA regarding your personal situation, whether it would be a good idea for you to contribute to Roth 401K.

Finally 401K has a profit sharing component that can provide an opportunity for significant contribution. We will not go over detail in this book, as my goal is just to get you familiar with your options. This is why, having a knowledgeable financial advisor on your team is essential for your wealth building successful strategy.

There are a great variety of retirement plans available for small business owners. Establish one for yourself by talking to your financial advisor to see what fits you and your business best and make regular contributions to it.

In my opinion, each business should have a retirement plan available to its employees as part of an incentive. It also helps stay more competitive on the labor market. Another reason for it would be to develop a strategy and discipline for securing your business owner's long-term financial success by funding it on a regular basis. When you run your business as an S-corporation you save money on payroll taxes, however, it will negatively affect your social security benefits when you are ready to retire. This is another reason why contributing to your own retirement plans is always a good idea.

Doing it consistently is also a key. For example, our office has Simple IRA plan, and I personally contribute at the maximum on a monthly basis as well as make extra tax payments with my check. Small amounts on a consistent basis will not affect your cash flow significantly, but will add up and make a significant difference at the end of the year. Consistent, small steps in the key to building wealth.

Now, let's talk about your individual retirement plans.

Employees and Retirement Plans

If you are an employee of the company, you can also utilize your offers via your job. Many companies offer matching up to 3% or so if you contribute money from your paycheck. When you leave your employment, you can roll the money from your employee-established 401K or 403B plans to your individual retirement account, called a Rollover IRA (which can be either traditional or Roth).

If you are a W-2 employee and a retirement plan is available for your contribution and matching by your employer from your job, utilize it! Tax deferred contributions, such as 401K, Simple IRA plans, as well as others, not only help you with tax savings in the current year but provide investment opportunities for your future. In addition, they allow you to earn more money from your employer (free cash!) and work towards your goal of increasing your financial net worth. Don't underestimate the value of your retirement plan contributions. If possible, maximize your contributions and don't plan to withdraw the money as it will not only create close to 25-40% taxable income rate (early withdrawal penalties are taking into consideration) but will also destroy the momentum of building your financial net worth.

Many clients ask me if they should contribute to a Roth IRA in addition to a Roth 401K investment vehicle, and I would say that it depends on your age, income tax bracket, and your legacy planning.

However, I always recommend to contribute money to your children's Roth IRA if they work for you and have earned income!

Contributing Money to Your Children's Roth IRAs

If your child of under 18 years of age works for you, and if your business is taxed as an LLC (not an S-corporation), then their paycheck can not only reduce your taxes (it is called an income shifting opportunity), but children's income up to $12,000 (new tax law standard deduction) is also tax-free and $6,000 can be contributed to a Roth IRA. Since Roth IRA accounts are tax-free and earnings generated inside these plans are tax-free (as they are funded with after-tax dollars), paying your children under $12,000 per year from your unincorporated business creates no taxable income for them and thus lets them contribute money to a Roth IRA. Since your children have earned income, they would qualify for Roth IRA contribution and pay no taxes on earnings. Your kids can withdraw the money from the Roth IRA to pay for education, finance their first home, or leave the money on the account to accumulate earnings tax free until they are ready to retire. This will provide an excellent opportunity to multiply their earnings since their contributions will start at a very early age and will have the opportunity to double their investments several times. Have you heard about the 8th wonder of the world, according to Albert Einstein? If not, it is called compound interest!

"Compound interest is the eighth wonder of the world."
—Albert Einstein

 Action Plan for Your Children's Roth IRA
Consider contributing money to your children's Roth Individual Retirement Account.

In order for them to qualify, they must have earned income, which will be satisfied by working for your business and issuing them a W-2 form. People that are under 18 years of age are not subject to FICA tax or FUTA. If you pay them up to their standard deduction of $12,000, they will not be subject to income tax either. The limit of Roth IRA contribution will be the smaller of their earned income or $6,000. Discuss your situation with your financial advisor and start contributing the money from their paycheck right away!

Paying your children and taking a tax deduction for it is a highly audited area. Make sure you have employee contract with them, list their job duties, keep track of their time at work and pay them a reasonable salary or hourly rate. Keep all records in case you get audited. Don't be afraid to utilize this tax strategy just because it increase your audit risk. Keeping your children employed not only saves you money on taxes, but teaches them work ethics and family business!

Traditional or Roth IRAs

Individual Accounts such as Roth or Traditional IRAs are available for individuals with earned income or even if only one spouse works.

If you have earned income in the year and was not covered by any retirement plan through an employer at some point, then you can contribute $6,000 (or $7,000 if you are over 50) (numbers for 2018-2019) into your Individual Retirement Account. Traditional IRA contributions are tax deductible if you or your spouse have no other retirement plans available. If you do, then depending on how much your earned income is, it can be either tax deductible or non-deductible. Your non-deductible

Traditional IRAs can be converted to a Roth IRA later on if needed. It is fairly common for individuals with high earnings to contribute to a non-deductible IRA and then convert it into Roth IRA. Talking to a tax professional is essential before you decide to convert your Traditional, non-deductible or even deductible IRA into Roth as it might trigger unnecessary taxes. For example, if you also have a SEP IRA, it will be taking into consideration when calculating taxes on conversion. Also, right timing would be when your income is low, or when you obtained credits, especially non-refundable tax credits. For example if you got adoption credits, solar credits, business tax credits, or others. Here's an example situation: you are lucky enough to have youth on your side but don't make a lot of money (thus in the lower tax bracket)—in this case, I definitely recommend that you open and start contributing to a Roth IRA. Earnings from a Roth IRA are tax free (which are calculated depending on your contributions, not your earnings) and distributions are tax free and penalty free, with a few exceptions that apply. However, once you start making more money, you will not be eligible to contribute straight to that Roth IRA, except if utilizing conversion options.

Always work with professionals in regard to your investing and always think about your future by taking action in the right direction. Something like making small contributions to your retirement

"Keep in mind that consistency is key in all areas of life, not just investing!"

accounts on a consistent basis could help you out a lot in the long run. Contribute on a regular basis and not just when the market is right or wrong. Keep in mind that consistency is key in all areas of life, not just investing!

You can also contribute money to your IRA (Individual Retirement Account) plans such as Traditional and Roth. Again, depending on your income and the availability of other retirement plans, your Traditional IRA contributions might or might not be tax deductible. Similarly, depending on your income, you might not even qualify to contribute to Roth IRA plans. You do not have to own a business to be able to contribute money to IRA accounts, but you or your spouse (if filing a "married filing jointly" tax return) should have earned income of at least the amount of the contribution.

Action Items:

1. Make an appointment with your financial advisor to discuss all of your options, your eligibility status, your contributions limit, and other unique considerations.

2. Plan for contributions limits by saving cash as well as contributing on a monthly basis.

3. Set up an automatic withdrawal from your personal bank account to contribute some money to your IRAs every month.

CHAPTER 7

Implementing Smart
Tax Strategies

TAXES ARE the highest expense everyone pays after they have earned their money. Strategic, consistent and intentional tax savings plans should be utilized on a monthly basis by smart entrepreneurs. This chapter is an overview of strategies that can be used by small business owners. It also states what type of taxes business owners must pay.

In my opinion, to declare their tax liability, business owners end up paying at least 10% less in income taxes, due to the fact that some of the expenses are paid by the employees after they already paid taxes. Business owners can deduct some of the expenses first and then pay taxes on what is left. However, when it comes to the IRS April 15th deadline, some business owners complain about having to pay taxes. This is because some of them don't pay taxes throughout the year with every paycheck they took, (like all employees and business owners should) and most of the time end up owing several thousand dollars on April 15th.

I cannot say this is the case for all business owners, however, as some entrepreneurs are very disciplined and regularly pay their estimated tax payments. Estimated tax payments should be paid in four equal installments that are due on April 15th, June 15th, September 15th, and January 15th of the following year. They also must pay payroll taxes on a bi-weekly, monthly or quarterly basis (depending on payroll tax liability amounts). Payroll taxes are the most strict taxes, as 10% failure to make timely deposits will apply, and penalties can be up to 100% when the IRS tries to collect back taxes, as they are not dischargeable in bankruptcy!

Personal Income tax liability can negatively interfere with business cash flow. Therefore, make a decision to pay all your calculated and projected tax liability throughout the year. Make sure it is also reflected in your cash flow forecast and budget.

Now, let's discuss your business taxes in detail.

Income Taxes

Whether you are a business owner or an employee, your share of payroll taxes needs to be withheld and paid in equal estimated tax installments, via payroll withholdings or a combination of both. Failure to do that will cause you to pay penalties and interest on outstanding tax liability balance. This becomes even more frightening if your business activities start to slow down and there is no cash to pay all of your taxes by the due date. It is always a good idea to have an available line of credit but it is not a good idea to owe all of that money on it.

It can be difficult on your cash flow to pay all of your tax liability at once by April 15th. Some business owners cannot afford to make their total tax payment at once and end up filing an extension on their tax returns. While it may sound like a quick fix, filing for an extension to file your tax return does not mean you are given an extension to pay. Therefore, when you owe money, you need to pay your tax liability by April 15th. Failure to do so will result in a penalty and interest accumulation. Now you see how essential it is to plan for your tax liability in advance, which I recommend to do at the beginning of the year. This topic applies to federal income and state tax withholdings and is applicable to business owners as well as your employees.

FICA Taxes—Social Security and Medicare Taxes

If you have a team of employees, or even just you (which still classifies as an employee), you are responsible for matching payroll tax withholdings as dictated by the Federal Insurance Contribution Act (FICA) taxes. This is a 7.65% tax. FICA programs include Social Security, Medicare and unemployment insurance. Failure to make accurate contributions or timely submission taxes to the IRS can result in significant tax penalties, an audit by the Internal Revenue Service (IRS), as well as potential bank levies. An audit brings significant downtime to your business plus runs the risk of financial or legal penalties if the IRS deems you did not make sufficient tax payments. Dealing with the IRS is not the best experience you can have especially when you have a tax liability. Therefore, payroll taxes should be one of your priorities to pay.

If you run payroll in your business, the best way to catch up on estimated taxes would be to pay an estimated tax liability via payroll. If tax payments (Federal and State income tax withholdings) are made through tax withholdings, the IRS treats these payments as if they were made in equal installments throughout the year. It can simplify the payment and recording process from time to time; however, this practice should not be a part of your tax strategy on a regular basis. You should always pay yourself a salary and submit a tax payment on a monthly or quarterly basis. This makes the financial burden of such taxes less noticeable and aids in ensuring the accuracy and timeliness of tax payments.

When calculating income tax deductions, consider income that will be flown into your individual tax return as net income from your S-corporation and plan for that income to cover its tax liability. Consult your CPA for estimated tax payment amounts.

Also, paying estimated tax payments should be a normal procedure for business owners. These estimated tax payments should be paid in equal quarterly installments (using forms 1040-ES) by April 15th, June 15th, September 15th and January 15th. Tax liability for estimated tax payments is calculated based on last year's tax liability. If last year's Prior Adjusted Gross Income was $150,000 or less, you can pay 100% of last year's income liability to avoid "failure to make" estimated tax payment penalties. If you choose to pay 100% of the previous year's income liability, you divide that amount into four quarterly installments. If your current-year adjusted gross income is more than $150,000, you can leverage the Safe Harbor Rule for minimum tax payments. The Safe Harbor Rule requires business tax payers in this bracket to pay 110% of your tax liability from the last year to avoid a penalty.

The IRS will provide you with Form 1040-ES to calculate and pay your estimated taxes. As we've previously covered, estimates are based on the previous year's tax liabilities but will be applied to the current fiscal year. The Form 1040-ES includes a dedicated worksheet to help you determine your estimated tax payments; your CPA can also complete these calculations on your behalf, after he or she completes your current year tax return.

Your estimated tax payments are due quarterly. If you've filed a tax extension for the current year and did not file your individual tax return by April 15th, most likely your CPA did not provide you with estimated tax payment vouchers for next year since no tax liability was available. Be sure to start making estimated tax payments by April 15th or pay an estimated tax liability via payroll to ensure that your estimated tax payments for next year are done in a timely manner. Either way you choose, make sure to make your estimated tax payments timely and in full.

If you run your business as an S-corporation, you can catch up on Federal and State income tax liability via payroll. Shareholders of the S-corporation must have payroll (for a reasonable salary) and must pay payroll taxes on it. Just increase your payroll Federal and State Income Tax Withholdings.

Action Items:

1. Ask your CPA to generate your estimated tax liability payment vouchers when he or she prepares your tax return. Pay attention to the penalties as well as interest you might have to pay with the return. As we discussed, there can be penalties for failure to make estimated tax payments, but there can also be a penalty for failure to pay your full tax liability for the previous year by April 15th. Always file an extension and timely tax returns (with extensions) as you might incur a failure to file penalty, which is up to 25% of your tax liability! Ouch!

2. If you had overpayment in the previous tax year, apply it toward your estimated tax payments versus asking for a refund.

3. **Review your W-4 form and amounts withheld on a regular basis.** Make sure to put 0's for exceptions if you make more money than what's just on the W-2.

4. If you don't have the funds to pay your tax liability, it is highly advised to file your tax return timely, with or without an extension and deal with the tax liability later, after filings. The penalty for failure to file, with or without an extension, is the most expensive penalty.

Never underestimate the power of the IRS and its collection procedures. The IRS collection procedures are something we should adapt to, because they will get their money from you. Always be careful about payroll taxes, pay them timely, as well as income taxes.

Have You Considered a Reclassification of Your Business Entity for Tax Purposes?

Many business owners start their businesses as a single-member LLC or a sole-proprietorship. But as they grow, those classifications might not make as much sense as they once did. When your business makes more than $30,000 in net income, it is a great time to think about entity reclassification. There are certain rules that must be followed and therefore, it is strongly recommended that you consult with a professional to help you with the reclassification of your business.

Income from S-corporations is not subject to the self-employment tax, which currently stands at a rate of 15.3%. Therefore, switching to an S-corporation can be very beneficial in the long run. However, there are a few rules that must be followed to avoid any problems with the IRS.

First of all, if you make money from your business and take draws (shareholder distributions), you must have a reasonable salary. A reasonable salary means that your S-corporation runs payroll for yourself and treats you as an employee. Payroll is also required for your spouse if he or she has an active role in your business. Your salary will be the only amount that is subject to self-employment taxes. Your income does not have to be comprised solely of a fixed salary. The IRS allows you to take 50% of the income from your S-corporation as a salary and 50% as a shareholder's distribution. The shareholder's distributions are not subject to SE (Self-Employment) tax. They also do not decrease your net income from your business. Shareholder distributions decrease equity (financial interest) in your business.

A lot of my clients ask me, if I take money from my business as shareholder distributions, will I be paying taxes on that amount? The answer for this is that you will be paying taxes on the net income from your S-corporation, not the movements of the cash itself. If you had cash to take from your business, it means that, with the exception of loans, your business made money. Otherwise, how did you come up with the cash in the bank? Whether you keep the money on the business bank account or take it to your personal account, you will pay taxes on the net income from your business. Of course, it is much better to have the money in the bank, so you will have money to pay these taxes when they come up.

If you've recently converted your business into an S-corporation, effective January 1st 2019, it is strongly suggested that you run the official payroll for yourself at least by December 31st 2019. I also recommend that you pay additional income taxes with your payroll to avoid penalties for not making your estimated tax payment in timely, quarterly payments (if applicable). I suggest to start running payroll when you make a decision to become an S-corporation—when you officially file Form 2553 with the IRS and state that you have intent to run your business as an

S-corporation. Keep an eye out for the IRS letter within 60 days after Form 2553 is sent to the IRS stating your business election. You definitely want to keep this letter in your permanent business folder documents! What is nice is that filing Form 2553 is just a one-time process. Once the IRS grants your business S-election status, your business is treated for tax purposes as an S-corporation.

Keep close attention what date the IRS grants your business S-corporation status. You can also apply for a retroactive S-election by using Revenue Ruling 2013-30.

Payroll is essential to a growing business. Not having payroll can cause an IRS audit and reclassification of your entire shareholder distributions as salary. That means that your shareholders distributions will become *"Payroll is essential to a growing business."* subject to self-employment tax as well as other payroll taxes. Net income from an S-corporation is not subject to payroll taxes. This is why a lot of small business owners prefer to run their businesses as S-corporations to minimize taxes. Another benefit to becoming a salaried employee is to secure your future Social Security benefits. If you're not on payroll, the available wages subject to Social Security can be minimal to none at all. It will negatively affect your future Social Security collection. Therefore, we strongly suggest you open an individual retirement account, SEP, Simple IRA or other retirement account from your business. To ensure your long-term financial success, you should fully contribute to your established retirement account. As you may remember, we discussed the importance of building your net worth with the three-legged stool concept. Saving for retirement is one leg of this net worth stool, so take your retirement contributions seriously.

Action Items:

1. **Consult with your CPA about converting your business into an S-corporation.** Each situation is unique and therefore you need a professional to accurately assess your needs and provide tailored advice.

2. **Understand how classification will impact your taxes, income methods and retirement contributions.**

3. **Make plans for retirement based on your income method and personal goals.**

4. **If you do qualify for an S-Corporation election or if the IRS granted it to you already, set up payroll and start paying yourself a salary as a shareholder's salary.** It can be a little bit complicated and confusing, therefore, hire a professional payroll company to handle your payroll.

Prepaying for Your Business Expenses in Advance

Another simple, yet frequently missed opportunity to save money on taxes is by making pre-payments. You should be prepaying for your operating expenses as well as equipment purchases.

Have you considered pre-paying for things such as rent, professional fees, purchased office supplies, business travel expenses, advertising, telephone, utilities, bonuses to employees (must be reported on their paychecks!), client gift purchases, expenses from business parties or even scheduled business retreats?

Shifting some of your business expenses that you plan on making in year 2 (a.k.a. next year), to this year (year 1) can benefit you in the current year. By purchasing computer equipment or furniture, you can take a Section 179 tax deduction and deduct the entire cost in December of that same year. You can make purchases with a credit card or by taking out a loan. It does not matter how you pay for it, as long as the transaction takes place before the end of December and the asset is placed in service before the end of December.

This is not to be confused with pre-payments for inventory. Your inventory available for sale is a balance sheet item and therefore it is not a business expense deduction until it is sold. Purchasing more inventory at the end of the year will decrease your cash balance in the bank but will have no effect on your expenses. Increase in inventory will increase your assets, but not your tax liability!

Prepaying for expenses can work on both cash and accrual methods, but mainly it will affect the cash method taxpayers for tax purposes (which most small business owners are).

Action Items:

1. Go over your Accounts Payable report and see what expenses could be paid in December for January. Of course, pay all of your outstanding invoices first!

2. Analyze your cash flow before you make a decision to pay or pre-pay for additional expenses.

3. Go over your cash available and expense reports. Calculate your next year projections. (If you expect higher income next year, prepaying for expenses this year might not be a good idea.)

4. Calculate your business prepayment amount, apply it to your effective tax bracket, and see what tax savings it can generate.

Opening and Contributing to Your Children's College Savings

Are you planning to save money for your kid's college education? Here are a few options that are available to you as a business owner:

- You can contribute money into a State Sponsored 529 college plan and take a State tax deduction. Sometimes some State sponsored plans are not the best and you can only take your State income tax deduction.

- Coverdell ESA college plans are available for up to $2,000. These tax-advantage savings plans let you save money for qualified education expenses on behalf of a named beneficiary, such as your child. If you spend the saved principal and its earnings on qualified purchases, none of the deduction or its earnings are taxable. Qualified purchases include tuition, books, and room and board.

Another alternative I suggest is employing your children, paying them the maximum exemption of $12,000 a year, and placing those earnings into a Roth IRA. Contributing these non-taxable earnings into an after-tax Roth retirement account helps your child start investing early. Do you remember the power of compound interest? Think about the financial opportunities your child will have if they leave their Roth IRA untouched for an extended period of time. They can pay for college, buy their first home, or start accumulating wealth early on. This smart move can set your child up for a bright financial future.

Best Times for Converting Your IRA into a Roth IRA

Usually when you start your business, your income drops in that year. This would create a good tax strategy of Traditional IRA conversion into a Roth IRA. The first step would be to determine if you need a conversion into a Roth IRA in the first place. If you are close to retirement, knowing that your income tax bracket will be lower and you don't have enough in your retirement account to generate significant earnings to be concerned about their taxation, perhaps leaving all your money in a Traditional IRA would be a good choice. If your tax advisor or CPA recommends a conversion as a good option, then during times when your income is at the lowest, it would be a good option to convert your money (either Rollover 401K or Traditional IRA into Roth). Usually, younger couples do this when they expect children and one spouse does not work during that time. Plus, adding additional dependents means that child tax credit and dependent care expenses might help to minimize the tax liability on conversion. Please note that conversions from non-deductible traditional IRA to Roth IRA have no tax effect, unless you have other IRAs – SEP or Simple. Then this conversion can trigger a taxable event.

Talk to your financial advisor and your CPA to discuss the situation related to you individually.

Action Items:

1. Check your Traditional IRA balance at the end of the year.

2. Identify timing of events when your income will be lower than usual.

3. Discuss IRA conversion effects with your CPA and Financial Advisor.

Making a Goal to Purchase Your First or Second Rental Real Estate Property

This section will get you out of your comfort zone if you have never bought or even thought of purchasing real estate for investment purposes. Real estate ownership is not for everyone, as it can be complicated, especially if there is no handy man around. Working closely with business owners and real estate investors, I can assure you that this strategy is not for everyone.

On the other hand, I work with some real estate investors who are very proud and excited about their real estate portfolio. The majority of them own several different properties and even make a living out of it! They add that already positive cash flow as their main source of income. I can tell you for sure that these people have it made. I personally like real estate opportunities and plan to get more rental properties in the near future.

So why real estate? There are more benefits to having rental real estate properties than drawbacks:

- The leasee pays off your loan and builds equity in your real estate properties.
- Your rental real estate properties appreciate in value on an annual basis, thus increasing your net worth. In fact, if purchased during proper timing, it appreciates on average at 2-5% per year.

This generates income for you while giving you tax deductions via non-cash depreciation expenses (if you qualify). Remember I talked about the importance of having positive cash flow? When the analysis is done properly, you will be earning a little bit of cash every month. Residential rental properties have to be depreciated over 27.5 years. Depending on your income, this can create a tax deduction via non-cash depreciation expenses.

You can also treat your rental activities as a business and your family members as employees and deduct those expenses. You can even put it down as an investment expense as long as these are related to travel expenses needed to research the area of the purchase of new properties (which includes overseas expenses if applicable).

Before you buy a rental property, you should make sure you have enough funds for a down payment. Additionally, you might be required to have good credit, emergency money and calculations showing that your income property will generate positive cash flow from day one. Purchasing a real estate property is very similar to owning a business. There is a risk involved, cash needed, and work required. It should also be a long-term strategy to create net worth and have a favorable tax treatment should you decide to sell it in the future. Real estate diversifies your portfolio to safely increase your assets and net worth.

> *"Real estate diversifies your portfolio to safely increase your assets and net worth."*

Obviously, you need to educate yourself about when is a good time to buy, what is the rent in the area, what are the direct expenses related to the property ownership. You need to do your homework before you jump off the cliff.

So here is the action plan . . .

Action Items:

1. Sign up to your local real estate investment club to make connections, obtain courage and education on how to purchase rental real estate properties.

2. Make a decision to buy at least one rental property every 2-3 years.

3. Develop a plan on how you will do it. Here is what my plan would look like:

   a. Pay off debt in terms of credit cards, vehicle loans and business lines of credit. Discuss what debt needs to be paid off first for a better effect with the mortgage specialist. He or she will also run your credit report to see what else needs to be addressed first.

   b. Start saving money, as investment property requires at least a 20% down payment.

   c. Make calculations of what your payments and cash flow will be as to make sure your investment will generate positive cash flow.

   d. Consult your real estate agent on timeliness of purchase, when the market will be to your benefit, as well as details such as location and other items that should be discussed beforehand.

> e. Just do it! Don't let fear and doubt control you. I have clients who shared their regrets for not taking the risk and buying investment properties when they could.

Your investment portfolio should be diversified, consisting of real estate, business, and retirement accounts, as well as other financial assets. Without a combination of the above, you will not be able to become a successful investor. You cannot just simply save money. Money needs to be reinvested by using leverage, either using other people's time, or money.

Reviewing Your Local Taxes for Compliance and Licensing Requirements: Sales Tax, Use Tax, Occupational Privilege Tax (OPT)

When you do business in a particular area, check out your local tax laws and regulations on what is required to stay in compliance with local tax authorities. I always suggest to work with the local professionals as they are more familiar on local tax regulations.

For example, in Denver, Colorado, business owners earning $500 or more on a monthly basis should pay Denver Occupational Privilege tax.

If you did not pay sales taxes on office supplies or equipment (perhaps you bought them outside of your local State), you most likely still have to pay use tax. Use tax in Colorado is the same rate as sales tax. Use tax should be paid within 30 days after taxable equipment or supplies were obtained.

⟶ **Action Items:**

1. Check with your local CPA for all your local tax compliance needs.

2. Contact local tax authorities to learn more about local taxes. Some of them teach free classes on a regular basis.

Reviewing Your Insurance Policies

Owner's life and disability health insurance, auto liability, as well as workers' compensation insurance policies should be reviewed to ensure your needs are met. Your insurance policies require careful deliberation, as they can become a delicate balancing act of paying too much or running the risk of being underinsured. You may wish to work with a broker or insurance professional to bundle policies for greater savings.

If you have employees, you must have workers' compensation insurance. Please check with your State for particular instructions. Workers compensation policy is priced depending on the wages your employees receive. It is very common for insurance companies to conduct insurance audits on an annual basis to make sure wage reports for the insurance policy are in correlation with what is paid by the business.

If you are more than 10% shareholder / owner, you can exclude yourself from the policy. Even though sometimes it might seem like a good idea, it might not, depending on what type of work you perform. If you do physical work, such as roofing, plumbing or heavy construction, ask yourself, what is my risk of getting hurt at work? If your risk is high, get the insurance, even if you are not required to have it by the State!

Also, talk to your insurance broker regarding an umbrella insurance, especially if you own several rental properties.

Taking Physical Count of Your Inventory

This step is applicable if you work in the retail industry. It is important to verify the correct ending balance of inventory at cost. Doing a physical inventory count in your business helps determine current assets, verifies cost of goods sold, and measures work-in-progress (WIP) inventory. These elements can be applied to your income statement using the accounting equation to help identify gross profit. Counting your inventory also helps identify some not-so-nice aspects of business, such as mishandled inventory, waste, or theft. The process can be time-consuming and rather monotonous, as the business owner or employee has to physically count and record items and their value. You can help alleviate the demands of inventory management with the help of an electronic aid, such as a sophisticated point of sale (POS) system or dedicated inventory management software. That sounds like a laundry list, I know. But taking this kind of proactive approach carries numerous financial benefits for you and your business. If your business does not carry inventory, it is time to celebrate!

> **➤ Action Items:**
>
> 1. Conduct a business-wide stock take of your current inventory, valuate each item and record your findings.
>
> 2. Consider utilizing POS or another inventory handling software for your business.

Analyzing Your Business for its Fair Market Salary

This section can be a little bit confusing but this is an eye opening concept. So, please pay attention.

Most of us, entrepreneurs working in our businesses, tend to discount the value of our time. Many of us choose to work fifty to seventy hours per week, work weekends, early mornings and nights and often don't count our time as a working time. We create a lifestyle out of it. This is all honorable and fine until one day when we are ready to replace ourselves and the honest realization hits us. We never pay ourselves the fair market salary due to tax savings techniques. Not to mention, we can't count our time because we might not

"Our business numbers could be significantly skewed and we would not even realize it!"

even know exactly how much time we spent. Therefore, our business numbers could be significantly skewed and we would not even realize it!

People elect their business to be taxed as an S-corporation so they can pay themselves a "reasonable salary." Unfortunately, most of the time that salary is way below how much they should pay themselves, a tactic used to save money on self-employment taxes. Then they review their business net income and proudly pat themselves on the shoulder, congratulating themselves on the very healthy net income. "Oh, my net income is about 35%, I am doing great," they say. If you look closely to their income numbers, especially if these businesses are taxed as S-corporations, you would notice that the owner's salary compared to his or her time invested in the business is actually way below minimum wage. Oops! Once this realization hits, you also understand that your business numbers are useless, at least in terms of the net income and owner's salary.

Therefore, when I review business reports for S-Corporations, the very first step is to review the owner's salary and distributions. Why is this important? There are several reasons:

1. You need to see how much your business actually makes, provided you want to hire someone to replace your position. Will you be paying that person $25,000, $30,000 or $80,000 in salary? What is your reasonable market salary? How much is the difference between the salary you pay yourself and the market salary? Now take that difference and subtract it from your net income. How do you like your net income now? For example, let's examine a law firm, a sole attorney, practicing law in his business taxed as an S-corporation. His business generates $150,000

in gross revenue. He is not eager to pay another $6,000 in self-employment taxes, so he pays himself $30,000 in salary. His business net income generates another $50,000 in net income from which he takes $30,000 as a distribution and leaves about $20,000 or so in the business bank account. Looks good, right? The IRS is satisfied, or somewhat satisfied, 50/50% salary to distributions ratios are met, his wife works and makes $70,000, so $100,000 is enough for them to cover their living expenses. Life is good. His business generated $50,000 which is 30% of his gross revenue. Looks like a healthy business. Now, let's take a closer look. How much is the fair market salary for this attorney should he choose to hire someone else to replace himself? Is it $100,000 or $70,000? Let's say it is $90,000. What happened now? If he replaces his "reasonable salary" of $30,000 with $90,000 his business is actually losing money, as he lost more than $10,000 (payroll taxes will increase as well as insurance). His business actually lost the money! Ouch! This is the most misunderstood concept in the real small business world when it comes to S-corporations.

2. The second reason is compliance with the IRS rules regarding "reasonable" salary. This means that if you don't pay yourself a salary that would cover your living expenses, such as mortgage, but pay your mortgage from your business account (even worse, as it is related to a commingling funds issue), the IRS can audit your business

and reclassify your shareholders' distributions into a salary and will make you pay payroll taxes, plus interest and penalties. Your reasonable salary amounts should be discussed with your CPA to keep you away from trouble.

3. Smaller salaries can also prevent you from fully contributing to your retirement accounts, and thus hinder your goals of building wealth for the future by saving money on taxes in the current time.

4. Smaller salaries also affect future distributions for your Social Security Fund. When the time comes to collect on Social Security benefits, this will happen at a minimum.

Action Items:

1. Review your annual shareholders' salary for a reasonable amount with your CPA.

2. Create a budget and forecast for cash outflow and a projection for taxes and increase in your salary.

3. Adopt a long-term mindset for success.

Paying Your Children Under 18 Years of Age
If They Work for You

This was briefly discussed in earlier chapters but definitely worth repeating! While it may be hard to get your kids to help out around the house, having them pull their weight around the family business has some pretty significant tax benefits.

If you run your business as a sole proprietor or a single-member LLC, you can pay your children (under 18 years of age) a salary or hourly rate for their work. Children under 18 years of age will pay no taxes on wages and are tax exempt from FICA and FUTA taxes on their first $12,000 in earnings (in 2018) from the unincorporated business of their parents. This will leave you with at least 25-35% of savings in taxes. In addition, if the parent makes more than $200,000, the child could reduce an additional 0.09% Medicare tax for the employer-parent. The payroll tax filing process is very simple. You would have to issue form W-2 and an annual payroll report form such as form 944 and 940 with $0.00 on them.

Since this is such a lucrative tax benefit, it has been subject to abuse by some taxpayers—leading to much scrutiny by the IRS. Therefore, you should meticulously track the hours your children work, outline their job responsibilities and record money flow to show that they are truly employees in your company. These records may be requested if you are audited by the IRS. Wages should also be reasonable depending on the children's age and responsibilities.

Here is a $4,000 tax savings strategy example:

Bob is a self-employed consultant and is in the 15% income tax and 15.3% self-employed tax bracket, plus a 4.63% State income tax rate. His total tax rate is 34.93%. His daughter is still in high school and very interested in marketing. So, she helps him with the social media advertising. He paid his daughter, Diane, $11,900 per year.

Diane has a traditional IRA account, where she contributed $6,000 as well as $12,000 in a standard deduction. Her taxable income is:

Wages: $11,900
Traditional IRA: ($6,000)
Standard Deduction: ($12,000)
Taxable Income = $0
Tax: $0

Bob saved $11,900 * 34.93% = $4,056 in taxes

Since Diane is in the smallest tax bracket, I would actually suggest for her to contribute money into a non-tax deductible Roth IRA. She would not even pay anything in taxes and will start earning her Roth IRA tax free! She is only 17, so being in a Roth IRA is a good tax deduction as she has many years to generate significant earnings. With all of this, she will be tax free provided she takes the money after she's 59.5 years old.

> **Action Plan: Setting up Your Children as Employees**
>
> If you are planning to have your children work for you, do the following items:
>
> - Create a job description for your children's positions.
>
> - Create a schedule of work for them and track their hours.
>
> - Make them salaried or hourly employees in your payroll system and pay them regularly just like you would do for any employee in your organization.
>
> - File payroll reports at the end of the year and file your children's individual tax return, if applicable.

Don't underestimate this technique, as it not only helps to develop strong work ethic for your children, but also save you money on taxes and introduces your kids to investing and budgeting techniques. If you operate your business as an S-corporation, perhaps creating a family unincorporated business would be a good idea where you can transfer money as management fees and make payroll from there.

If you operate your business as a corporation or have children over the age of 18, don't be discouraged to utilize the same method of tax savings strategy. Your tax savings might not be that significant, but I am sure it will have a significant non-monetary effect on your family's work ethic. One day you might want to sell your business and the children might be interested in buying it.

CHAPTER **8**

Health Care and Taxes

HAVE YOU purchased or obtained your new health insurance plan? The world of healthcare and taxes has become intermingled and it is creating some new points of interest that every business owner should have on their radar come tax time.

Health Insurance for Business Owners

Have you purchased a health insurance plan for you and your employees via the Small

"Every business owner should have health insurance on their radar come tax time."

Business Health Options Program (SHOP) marketplace? The SHOP insurance marketplace is available to business owners with fewer than 50 employees. You can find more information on health insurance options at Healthcare.gov or through your private benefits provider.

Under the Affordable Care Act, the role of health insurance in the business world is more important than ever before. As you might know, penalties for not having health insurance are no longer applicable; however, having no health insurance can put you in significant risk of losing your financial assets should an emergency arise.

Business owners should exercise caution when taking money in advance for health insurance premiums. These are called health insurance assistance programs and the premium amount is based off of your estimated annual income. If your income is higher than predicted, you may be responsible for paying the difference of the premium back. It can be painful and difficult to calculate without the assistance of an expert. The best solution would be to wait until your tax returns are filed to see if you qualify in the first place. If you do qualify for the tax credit, you will receive it with your tax return. This is called an advanced health insurance tax credit. Either way, if you qualify for the advanced insurance payments, you will not lose them.

If you have an S-corporation and pay health insurance only to yourself, you can use it as a special tax deduction. This deduction will show up on page 1 of your individual tax return form 1040. In a way, your health insurance will reduce income for income tax purposes. However, in order for the IRS to allow you to take this deduction, your health insurance premiums should be recorded correctly on your W-2 form. Paid health insurance premiums will add to your officer's salary for income tax purposes and not

FICA (Social Security and Medicare purposes). Communicate this item to your payroll service provider to ensure everything is correctly recorded on your W-2 form. Your health insurance premiums will be deducted as a business expense. Because premiums are deducted, you can pay them through your business checking account or reimburse yourself for paying it personally. It is reported and deducted differently, in comparison to other business tax deductions, for tax purposes.

Action Items:

1. Pay for your health insurance premiums from your business checking account.

2. Instruct your payroll company to record the health insurance premiums paid on your W-2 form, as it is subject to Federal and State income tax but not FICA (Social Security and Medicare taxes). The health insurance premiums should be added to your Federal and State subject to income tax wages (not FICA) and the medical insurance premiums reports in Box 14 (Shareholder's health insurance).

3. If you have employees and offer them a health insurance benefits, you must have non-discriminatory group health insurance plan.

How does the IRS know if you had insurance for the year? Your health coverage information including advanced tax credits received, if applicable, is reported on either Forms 1095-A or 1095-B. The IRS uses a matching principle, just like any other form you receive, to see if you had a health coverage.

If you are fairly healthy, I would suggest to have a high deductible health insurance plan and open a Health Savings Account (HSA). Contributions to HSA are tax deductible above the line on page 1 of Form 1040 and the premiums will be less expensive versus other plans.

In our firm we have a group health insurance plan. I believe group health insurance plans not only provide a better coverage but also create your business more lucrative for employee hiring and retaining purposes.

Utilizing a Health Savings Account (HSA)

When you have a high deductible health insurance plan, you will most likely qualify for HSA contributions. An HSA uses pre-tax dollars to cover qualifying medical expenses. They are similar to a flexible spending account (FSA). But unlike an FSA, the balance in an HSA accrues year-after-year and is never forfeited if it goes unspent. Once you turn 65, you'll also be able to draw from your HSA penalty-free—even for non-qualifying medical expenses. But if you use the HSA for non-qualifying expenses before you turn 65, you will be subject to a 20% penalty plus it will be taxable income. If you have not opened an HSA account yet, please do so before December 31st to begin reaping the rewards of this tax advantage. You can contribute money into your account before April 15th of the next year, but the account must be open before January 1st of that year. As an example, the maximum contribution amounts for 2019 are $3,500 for individuals and $7,000 for family coverage. Those of age 55 or older can contribute an extra $1,000 per year. Your HSA plan remains unchanged, even if you switch health insurance providers. As long as you continue owning an HSA, you will be able to use and contribute to the same account.

Contributions to an HSA are deducted as an adjustment to your gross income line item for income tax purposes on page 1 of Form 1040. If you have your business set up as a Schedule C and your spouse or children work for you, but you have no other employees, you might be able to deduct health insurance premiums (provided health insurance plan is owned by your employee-spouse) as well as HSA contributions made as an ordinary business expense on Schedule C, just like an employee benefit. Before taking on this money-saving task you'll want to make sure that your employed spouse is truly an employee and not considered a business partner.

When you take the money from your HSA account to pay for your medical expenses, these medical expenses are not deducted on Schedule A or anywhere else on your tax returns. This is because your tax deduction was taken already when the HSA contributions were made. If you are under 65 and withdraw money from your HSA for any reason other than a qualifying medical expense, you'll be subject to 20% penalty. Distributions will also be subject to income tax. Unused money can be invested if needed and can work as a self-directed HSA account if you have significant investments there.

Action Plan: Your HSA Account

Open an HSA account by December 31st of the year when your high deductible plan was created. Even if you did not spend any money for your medical expenses in the previous year, still contribute the money, take a deduction and you actually have an option to invest your HSA money into the other investment vehicles. That way you will still have time to contribute and fully or partially fund your HSA by April 15th.

CHAPTER 9

Tax Deductions

BASED ON my experience with some business owners, I can tell that some of them do not feel comfortable taking some of the tax deductions they are entitled to. This can be due to being concerned about an increased audit risk, lack of understanding on how to calculate it, or just not being aware of certain rules. This chapter is about reminding or learning about these tax deductions so that business owners can positively affect their tax liability.

Purchasing Fixed Assets

Is your business growing? Do you need to purchase new fixed assets, such as a computer, technical equipment and even vehicles? December would be the ideal time to make those purchases.

Based on various depreciation deduction options, you can deduct the entire cost of your assets by using Section 179 tax deduction, provided your business has net income. If your business has net income, you can deduct the cost of computers or furniture entirely versus depreciating it over 5-7 years. You can also utilize bonus depreciation provided brand new assets were purchased.

It is important to use common sense when applying this trick, as it can be easy to get carried away in all the tax savings. Make sure you truly need something for your business and that you are not just buying it for tax deduction. Don't pay $1 to save $.30 cents. Long-term, strategic thinking is what sets successful business owners apart. Weigh the pros and cons of new capital investments in your business and make a decision based on needs, not wants. Remember, these fixed assets will increase your businesses' net worth, so it is a wise investment in your future.

"Make sure you truly need something for your business and that you are not just buying it for tax deduction."

When it comes to vehicles, tax depreciation laws are different. In order to deduct up to $40,000, your vehicles should be over 6,000 lbs., brand new, and must be used more than 50% for business purposes. You can use bonus depreciation and Section 179 of the tax law to maximize your depreciation tax deduction for tax purposes. Keep in mind though, especially if you have truck payments, that once you offset the majority cost of your truck in year one, and save taxes, you will have very minimal tax deduction left in the future years (or no tax deduction) but will continue experiencing cash outflows in terms of monthly truck payments without any tax benefits.

Another sad reality is if you decide to sell your auto, or for some unfortunate reason it is repossessed, most likely you will end up with a tax bill to cover the taxable income in terms of the difference between the book value of your truck (which will be close to zero after the bonus you received and Section 179 tax code depreciation you took) and the sale price of the vehicle.

Any tax strategy should be carefully considered and a long-term perspective should be applied. If you decide to depreciate your auto, you need to place the cost of the vehicle on the company's balance sheet account. Now you can take out the actual business expenses related to this vehicle. You can deduct gas, maintenance, truck insurance, repairs and other actual costs associated with the vehicle. Don't forget to prorate these expenses between business and personal use. If you use your vehicle for less than 50% of your business, you cannot take a depreciation expense, and if your vehicle usage drops to less than 50% you would also have to recapture all that depreciation taken. The same applies to your gas and oil, repairs and maintenance, insurance and other actual expenses—you have to take only a business use portion of it.

Another strategy would be to utilize a business mileage of your vehicle, compared to the actual expenses.

Calculating Your Business Mileage

When you use your regular listed vehicle, you might be better off by calculating the business mileage using a mileage log and multiply it by the amount per mile assigned by the IRS. The amount you can expense per business mileage varies every year and can be looked up on the **IRS.gov** website. For example, the cost of each business mile in 2019 is $0.58 per mile. You simply use your mileage log and multiply number of your business miles used by that amount.

When is it beneficial to calculate business mileage?

- When you have an inexpensive vehicle that you use less than 100% of the time for business.
- You drive a lot and work from home.
- When you sell that vehicle, you won't have to show income from the sale.
- Vehicles that are depreciated on the company books most likely have lower costs and the sale of such vehicles can cause income recognition.

Exceptions to the mileage rules are:

- When your business has a fleet—more than five vehicles on your businesses balance sheet.
- When you operate a freight truck (these can cost hundreds of thousands of dollars, and the actual expense must be taken into consideration).
- When you lease your vehicle; you can deduct its cost of the lease multiplied by the business use as well as actual expenses, such as fuel, maintenance, and taxes. Keep in

mind that the lease inclusion must be subtracted from the lease costs. These numbers are available from IRS tables and the amounts are not that significant.

Do not underestimate the fact that you are utilizing your vehicle for your business. This is especially true if you work from home. When you work from home, you have no commuting mileage and every time you leave your house for business, you should calculate your business mileage.

Keep in mind that by taking business mileage, you cannot take actual expenses related to your vehicle maintenance, such as gas and oil change, repairs, or car insurance.

You can however, take the loan interest expenses multiplied by the business use of your vehicle for both types of vehicle deductions. Parking and tolls are deducted without limitation and despite the type of vehicle expenses used.

You cannot switch to the standard mileage method if you started implementing the actual method in the previous year. Meaning, you cannot completely and significantly deduct the depreciation of the vehicle and then start taking business mileage, thus maximizing both methods. The IRS does not want you to have your cake and eat it too.

If you don't work from home and you actually drive to the office on a daily basis, it is called commuting and you are not eligible for business mileage deduction. Since your employees drive to your office without taking this expense as a tax deduction, why should you? You can, however, deduct your mileage when you drive for business either before or after your office time. So, open a P.O. Box for your business and check your mail every day before you go to the office. That way you can subtract your mileage driven to the office as business mileage!

Keeping a mileage log is very important and the IRS asks about it during their audits. Also, if you have two vehicles used by your business, then we recommend to use just one. Only use this one vehicle 100% of the time or close to it for business and keep the other vehicle for personal use. The IRS most likely will not allow you to deduct mileage from both vehicles if you are the only one involved in the business.

> *"Keeping a mileage log is very important and the IRS asks about it during their audits."*

How can you keep track of your miles? Use Apps such as MileIQ or others. You can use your calendar with your business activities and meetings. If you ever get audited the IRS will most likely ask you for your mileage log.

Taking a Home Office Deduction

Is the commute to your office just a 30-second walk from your bed? If so, there are many tax benefits at your disposal. More than half of all U.S. businesses are based out of an owner's home, according to the Small Business Administration. Many of these small business owners utilize their personal resources when working in their dedicated office space—these resources can be deducted to save money on their taxes. Unfortunately, due to negative opinions held by the IRS, an audit risk significantly

"More than half of all U.S. businesses are based out of an owner's home, according to the Small Business Administration."

increases if you take a home office deduction. It causes many people to be hesitant to deduct these major money-savers. If you truly utilize your space in your home for business, take your home office deduction!

You must meet three conditions before you can claim a home office:

- **Exclusive use:** your home office must be used exclusively for business purposes.
- **Regular use:** you must regularly use a dedicated space for your home office.
- **Business use:** this space in your home must be your principal place of business or used for face-to-face meetings with customers or clients on a regular basis.

Home Office Deduction Methods:

Starting as of 2013, you have two options for deducting home office expenses—regular and simplified.

Regular—this method involves determining the actual expenses of your home office and recording them. It requires far more calculations and record-keeping but there are some monetary benefits associated with this extra legwork. Shared expenses will be allocated based on the percentage of your home used for business. In this method, you have to include depreciation deductions for a portion of your home-related expenses. The amount in excess of net income limitations may also be carried over to the following fiscal year.

Regular business home office expenses are reported on Form 8829—Home Office Deduction. There is separation between direct (expenses directly attributable to your home office, such as painting done in the office) or indirect, expenses related to the entire house, with only a portion of it attributed to the home office. Mortgage interest, real estate taxes, house insurance, utilities cost—all of these expenses are related to maintaining the entire house and only a percentage of the business home office is deducted as a home office expense.

The regular method involves excess calculation and allocation that can be overly complex, especially for small business owners. You also have to take a depreciation expense on your house, which would result in a capital gain once you decide to sell your house. However, as the new law increased standard tax deduction to $12,000 (or $24,000 for married filing joint tax return), many taxpayers are not able to deduct their mortgage interest (as their new standard tax deduction is higher than their itemized tax deductions). In this case, I do recommend to take at least a fractional tax benefit of your mortgage interest payment. Besides, most of the time, utilizing actual home office tax deduction results in higher tax benefits.

The simplified method creates an easier expense process by allowing business owners to take the actual square footage of your office, up to 300 sq. ft. and multiply it by $5 per sq. ft. Therefore, the maximum tax deduction available to you would be $1,500. The good news is that the entire 100% of the mortgage interest and real estate taxes will be allocated to Schedule A, no depreciation expense would be needed, and thus no capital gain consequences will occur.

So, what method if the most advantageous, you might ask? The answer would be, it all depends! For 80% of the time, the regular method is more advantageous because more expenses allocated to the home office can help to offset your self-employment taxes. Let's examine the situation:

Let's say you have a small office that takes up about 200 square feet of your 2,000 square foot home. Since your office makes up 10% of your home, you'd expense 10% of these shared costs as business deductions.

Your home mortgage interest is: $7,000
Real Estate taxes: $2,500
Insurance: $1,500
Utilities: $2,800
HOA: $1,200
Depreciation: $10,000

Take 10% = $2,500

If you use the simplified method= $5 * 200 = $1,000

As you can see, by using a regular home office deduction you save $1,500 *15.3%=$230 more in SE taxes. When you use a home office, make sure to compare the two methods to see which one suites you the best.

Reviewing Your Travel and Meals Expenses to Maximize Tax Deductions

Travel, meals and entertainment are some of the hottest IRS audit buttons, but do not let that stop you from expensing these valuable business expenses. Wining and dining clients is just part of the job description for millions of Americans. These are key relationship-building activities that are instrumental in taking our business to the next level. With that said, it's important to utilize these luxuries appropriately and keep thorough record of business-related outings.

- Travel—the IRS has strict rules regarding travel-related business deductions. In order to be expensed, travel deductions must be as a result of "necessary expense" for being away from your home for business, job or profession. For tax purposes, your "home" is an all-encompassing term for the city or general area in which you live. Travel by car can be deducted by standard mileage rates, as set by the IRS. You can also deduct the cost of lodging, taxi fare, airport limo, baggage and shipping, dry cleaning and laundry and even tips incurred while traveling.

- When it comes to meals, you can deduct the cost of meals purchased while traveling. The requirements are that it must be outside of your city and you can only deduct 50% of the unreimbursed cost of your meal.

- Entertainment—the IRS has very different views of entertainment than you or I. Indeed, they completely disallowed it starting in 2018!

Shifting Your Itemized Deduction on Your Individual Tax Return Due to Higher Standard Tax Deduction

Analyze your itemized deductions on Schedule A of your individual tax return and put them to work for you. With the New Tax Act and Jobs Act of 2017, the new standard tax deduction is $12,000 if single, $18,000 of head of household and $24,000 for married filing joint tax returns.

There is a new $10,000 limit of all taxes paid in the previous years. Meaning, your total State Income tax, personal property tax, real estate tax and other local taxes, are limited to $10,000 only. Your mortgage interest is tax deductible on the loans up to $750,000 only.

There are no unreimbursed employee tax deductions allowed. Your charitable contributions are limited to 60% of your AGI (Adjusted Gross Income), which used to be 50%. It will not affect the majority of people.

Based on a new much higher standard tax deduction, shifting expenses can be a very popular strategy now. You might not be able to shift some items, such as income tax withheld from your W-2, but items such as charitable contributions, real estate taxes and even mortgage interest prepayments are feasible to shift. Again, this strategy will only be applicable for some taxpayers. If you are new to house ownership, most likely you are at the beginning of the amortization schedule and therefore, it would not make a difference for you.

For taxpayer with RMD (Required minimum distributions), contributing to a charity from their IRA can be a very good tax saving strategy as they will not show income from IRA distributions.

Again, each situation is different and working closely with your CPA can guarantee you some tax savings!

Action Item

Review your prior year's tax return and discuss your itemized deduction shifting strategy with your CPA.

CHAPTER 10

Conclusion

THE SUCCESS of your business is dependent on how much good intention you put into it. Pay attention to your numbers, compare them to your projections, evaluate your non-financial business opportunities, evaluate your employees, and work to predict your long-term success.

Remember, building a business is a marathon, not a sprint. I would like to remind you to continue intentionally working with other professionals. They can enlighten you with advice if they have done this themselves. Maybe they have the experience and have seen the challenges other clients have faced in the past. They could also just be more acquainted with best practices and how to effectively implement

"Remember, building a business is a marathon, not a sprint."

them. How can you tell if you have selected the right professionals for your team? Interview them, ask them to share their personal experiences, and evaluate their mindset—is it similar to yours, are you sharing the same core values and beliefs about the business experience? What do they struggle with at work? What are their best practices and abilities for the business?

I also suggest to find similarly-minded entrepreneurs to share your business practices with, add them to your list of networks and make an effort of meeting them quarterly.

Also, don't sell yourself short. Consider offering your services in a bundle or packaged deal. Our CPA firm has created special offers in terms of three different types of packages to offer to our growth-minded entrepreneurs. This makes the decision to come onboard with us much easier for the client and is also easier for our employees to handle.

Selecting Your CPA to Guarantee Business Success

As the book comes to an end, we would like to discuss the last topic on how you can work with a CPA firm to achieve business success. Make sure you make a list of key factors to look for when choosing your CPA. A CPA firm just like ours might end up being the perfect choice for you. Since any new topic in business can be very confusing, allow us to tell you a little bit about what we offer at our firm.

We offer three different packages for our clients that satisfy all compliance needs for the IRS and we also go beyond that, helping our clients fulfill their strategic needs. We work with business owners throughout the country, specializing in service-based businesses that are intentional to take their business to the next level. Please refer to our website at **www.ColoradoBusinessCPA.com** for more information.

Thank you for investing your time learning more about how to create a successful business by being intentional about its growth, income, and expenses. We wish that you keep learning, growing, and inspiring others! Also, remember to share your best practices with fellow entrepreneurs, as we all rise by lifting others.

Sincerely,
Natalya Itu

Section 199A Tax Deduction

TAX CUTS and Jobs Act of 2017 enacted a very beneficial tax deduction for business owners, called Section 199A tax deduction.

Based on that Qualified Business Income Deduction, pass-through entities may be able to deduct 20% of their business net income as an ordinary business tax deduction. For example, if your business net income was $100,000; you might be able to take 20% of it, which is $20,000 as a business tax deduction, resulting in tax savings somewhere from $2,000 to $8,000, depending on your ordinary tax rate bracket!

Who would qualify?

Pass-through entities, such as Sole Proprietors, LLCs, Partnerships, S-corporations, trusts and estates, REITs (Real Estate Investment Trusts) and Qualified Cooperatives.

There are two different types of categories (depending on which your business operates under and your level of taxable income) that can be applicable to you. This will determine whether you will qualify for a tax deduction or not.

Specified Service Trade or Business (SSTB) are businesses such as doctors, attorneys, accountants, actuaries, consultants, artists, athletes, anyone who works in the financial services or brokerage industries, and when the principal asset of the business is reputation and skills of the owner.

Unfortunately, if your business falls under this type of category, you have income limitations to apply your 20% qualified business tax deduction.

If your taxable income is under $157,500 (single) and $315,000 (married), then you can apply the 20% tax deduction.

If your taxable income is between $157,500 to $207,500 (single) or $315,000 to $415,000 (married), your deduction will be limited.

And of course, if your taxable income is more than $207,500 or $415,000, no qualified business tax deduction will be available to you.

When your business does not fall under SSTB (Specified Service Trade or Business), your calculations will be the following:

If your taxable income is under $157,500 (single) and $315,000 (married), then you can apply the 20% tax deduction.

If your taxable income is between $157,500 to $207,500 (single) or $315,000 to $415,000 (married), the QBI deduction cannot exceed the greater of 50% of W-2 wages or the sum of 25% of W-2 wages plus 2.5% of the tangible property.

And if your taxable income is more than $207,500 or $415,000, partial QBI deduction will be available to you.

Your real estate investment activities might also qualify for a QBI tax deduction, provided your treat it as business, especially for real estate professionals.

In general, Section 199A tax deduction (by the way, it is shown on your individual tax return, not business), is one of the greatest tax benefits that became available. Careful analysis of your particular situation would be required as well as planning to maximize that deduction for future years.

Working with your CPA will ensure the maximizing of your tax benefits. Please feel free to contact us with your questions as we are passionate about helping growth-minded entrepreneurs succeed in this confusing world of taxation and business in general!

Appendix

Table 1: Net Worth and Action Plan

Asset Name	Fair Market Value (FMV)	Debt Outstanding	Annual Cash Inflow/ Outflow	Is it a Necessary Debt?	Improvements Needed and Results

Clarifying Insights:

_____

_____

_____

_____

"Aha!" Moment Reflection: Do you have Liabilities or Assets?
Do you have a business or a job?

_____

_____

_____

_____

_____

_____

Action steps needed to improve your financial position by the
end of the year?

_____

_____

_____

_____

Table 2: Business Scorecard / Financial Net Worth

(Balance Sheet and Action Steps)

Assets / Description	As of Today	Ideal Picture	Action Steps
Cash			Save cash $_____
Accounts Receivable			Improve Collections by ____% or $_____
Fixed Assets (Net)			Invest in new office equipment $_____
Other Notes			
Liabilities			
Short-Term Debt			
Long-Term Debt			Pay off $_____ by 12/31/_____
Equity			Increase by $_____
Sales			Increase by $_____
Expenses			Decrease by $_____
Owners Payroll			Reasonable Salary
Net Income			Increase by $_____

Action Steps to Implement and Accomplish Goals from "Ideal Picture" Column:

_____

_____

_____

_____

_____

_____

_____

_____

_____

_____

_____

_____

_____

_____

Table 3: The Non-Financial Assets of Your Business

Asset Description	FMV of the Assets	Projected Potential Results	Improvements Needed
The Team			
Company's Culture			
Systems / Processes			
Marketing / Sales			
Hours Owner Worked			
Cumulative Experience of Team			
Unique Ability of the Team			
Reputation on the Market			
Growth Trend			
Customers/ Clients List			

Action Steps to Improve Your Company's Position on the Market:

_____

_____

_____

_____

_____

_____

_____

_____

_____

_____

_____

_____

_____

_____

_____

_____

_____

Table 4: Unsecured Debt

Many of us have debt, and some of it is unsecured. If your credit cards were used to pay for business expenses, your tax advantage was already used. Therefore, paying for the debt as soon as possible can be a good idea otherwise it will only slow the business growth. Same concept will apply for your personal debt. So, let's make a list of all your unsecured debt and develop an action plan to get rid of it for good!

"Never own anything that eats while you sleep."

—Dan Sullivan, Strategic Coach®

Unsecured Debt Description	Total Amount of Debt	Payments - Cash Outflow on a Monthly Basis	Why Did You Accumulate This Debt?	Pay The Debt Away Deadline

Clarifying Moment – Action Plan to Diminish Unsecured Debt:

_____

_____

_____

_____

_____

_____

_____

_____

_____

_____

_____

_____

_____

_____

_____

_____

_____

Table 5: Non-financial Assets that are Confidence Boosters

Description of the Asset	How Can These Confidence Boosters Improve My Life?	Potential Earnings for Next Year	Potential Earnings for the Next Five Years
Education/ Certifications			
Knowledge			
What I'm really good at			
Upcoming Exciting Projects			
Experience			

Action Steps to Improve My Life:

_____

_____

_____

_____

_____

_____

_____

_____

_____

_____

_____

_____

_____

_____

_____

_____

_____

Table 6: Building a Team for Long-Term Success

Creating great relationships with people results in an exciting and successful life in the long-term. These relationships require attention and intention on a regular basis. This table will give ideas about who you want to invite into your success team and what actions are needed to improve your relationships.

Professions	Person Name	Help Needed With	Contact Information	Next Meeting Scheduled
Business Attorney		Contracts		
Real Estate Attorney		Real Estate Investments		
Estate/ Trust Attorney		Estate Planning		
CPA		Business Finances / Taxes		
Financial Advisor		Retirement Plans/ Life / Disability Insurance		
Business Banker		Banking / Loans		
Real Estate Agent		Investments in RE		
Loan Officer/ Mortgage Broker		RE Investments		
Insurance Broker		Insurances (workers compensation, health, cars, other liabilities, etc.)		

Professions	Person Name	Help Needed With	Contact Information	Next Meeting Scheduled
Business Coach		Clarity, Direction, Business Improvements		
Business Broker		Business Valuation, Business Exit Strategy or Purchase of a New Business		
Bookkeeper/ CPA		Bookkeeping/ Tax Planning		
Payroll Processor/ CPA		Payroll Compliance		
Collection Agent		Collections from Customers		
HR Person		Employee Issues		

Have regular meetings with your team members. Also, depending on your industry, identify people that can be referral partners (people who can refer business to you and you can refer business back to them). Add them to your list and make regular, intentional meetings with them so that they may remain in your success team as long as possible.

ScoreCards for your Business

If you want to know if your business is doing well and on track of achieving its goals, your business need to have a ScoreCard. I would recommend to select up to ten Key Performance Indicators (KPIs) so you can easily credit if your business is on track or not. At my firm, we select weekly performance indicators for each member. These are amount of billings, amount of weekly collections, Accounts Receivable (ARs) weekly ending balance, number of new clients and marketing actions. Key Performance Indicators allow business owners to determine a lot of information in a short period of time. Are you on track of achieving your goals?

Table 7:
Determining Your Main Key Performance Indicators (KPI)

Description of KPI	Weekly Goal	Actual Weekly Numbers	Year to Date Total	Is There A Discrepancy?
Production/ Sales				
Amounts collected				
New Customers				
Bank Balance				
Short Term Debt				

Action Steps to Improve Discrepancies:

_____

_____

_____

_____

_____

_____

_____

_____

_____

_____

_____

To Your Success!

About the Author

Natalya Korobkova-Itu, CPA is an entrepreneur at heart. She never stops learning about other business owners' best practices and strives to be a better business owner herself. She came to the USA from Russia in 1998 with her mother, very little money, and no English language skills. Despite those circumstances, her strong will and resilient nature makes her an inspiration to many. She thrives in showing others the power of being intentional and how it can help take  them wherever they want to be in life. As a long time business owner, she shares her best practices from experience and constantly strives to uplift, inspire, and help guide entrepreneurs to success.

She has been a Colorado-licensed CPA for over eight years and an accountant for over twelve years. Her CPA firm, **ColoradoBusinessCPA.com** is located in Englewood, Colorado and specializes in offering business packages including tax, accounting, payroll, and coaching support for small business owners.

When she is not at her desk, she enjoys hiking with her rescued Labradors, traveling the world, reading many books, exercising, and dining out with her family and friends.